Virtual Real Estate Gold

Unveiling the Wholesaling Secret in the Digital Age

JEFFREY S LOOMIS

Copyright

Table of contents

Dedication

In humble gratitude to Almighty God, whose boundless grace illuminates our paths and blesses our endeavors, I offer this work. To the One who bestows wisdom and guidance, thank you for the inspiration that fuels our journey into the realms of Virtual real estate Gold. This book is dedicated to the fearless entrepreneurs and digital pioneers who dare to venture into uncharted territories. Your relentless pursuit of innovation and your unwavering commitment to excellence serve as beacons of inspiration to us all.In particular, this dedication is extended to those who seek to uncover the wholesaling secrets within the digital landscape. Your determination to unravel the mysteries of virtual real estate and harness its potential for prosperity is commendable. May the insights shared within these pages serve as a guiding light, empowering you to navigate the ever-evolving world of virtual real estate with confidence and clarity. Jeffrey S. Loomis gratefully dedicates this work to the bold visionaries who illuminate the path to success in the digital age.

Author Bio

Jeffrey S. Loomis is a seasoned entrepreneur, visionary strategist, and leading authority in the dynamic field of virtual real estate. With a passion for innovation and a keen eye for emerging trends, Jeffrey has dedicated his career to uncovering the hidden potential within the digital landscape. Drawing from his extensive experience in real estate wholesaling and digital marketing, Jeffrey brings a unique perspective to the realm of virtual real estate. His forward-thinking approach and unparalleled insights have positioned him as a trailblazer in the industry, pioneering new strategies for success in the digital age. Jeffrey's journey into virtual real estate began with a relentless pursuit of knowledge and a commitment to excellence. Through years of hands-on experience and continuous learning, he has honed his expertise in identifying lucrative opportunities and capitalizing on emerging trends. As the founder of several successful ventures in the virtual real estate space, Jeffrey has earned a reputation for his innovative strategies and proven track record of success. His ability to navigate the complexities of the digital landscape with precision and foresight has earned him the respect and admiration of peers and colleagues alike. In **"Virtual Real Estate Gold: Unveiling the Wholesaling Secret in the Digital Age,"** Jeffrey shares his wealth of knowledge and expertise, offering readers a comprehensive guide to unlocking the full potential of virtual real estate. With practical insights, actionable strategies, Jeffrey empowers readers to navigate the digital terrain with confidence and achieve unprecedented success in the world of virtual real estate. Whether you're a seasoned investor looking to expand your portfolio or a newcomer eager to explore the possibilities of virtual real estate, Jeffrey S. Loomis's expertise and guidance will prove invaluable on your journey to success in the digital age.

Introduction

Welcome to the Groundbreaking world of virtual real estate wholesaling! In **"Virtual Real Estate Gold**: Unveiling the Wholesaling Secret in the Digital Age," Jeffrey S Loomis takes you on an eye-opening journey into the lucrative realm of digital property trading. Whether you're a seasoned real estate professional or a novice investor, this book is your essential guide to mastering the art of virtual wholesaling and leveraging the power of the digital age to unlock unprecedented opportunities.

By delving into "Virtual Real Estate Gold," you will:

★ Gain a comprehensive understanding of the virtual real estate market and its potential for exponential growth.

★ Uncover the insider secrets and strategies for effectively wholesaling virtual properties in the digital landscape.

★ Learn how to identify and capitalize on emerging trends and untapped niches within the virtual real estate market.

★ Acquire practical tips for navigating the legal and logistical aspects of virtual property transactions.

★ Harness the latest technology and digital platforms to maximize your virtual real estate wholesaling endeavors.

<u>By not investing in "Virtual Real Estate Gold," you'll be missing out on:</u>

★ Invaluable insights that could propel your real estate investment ventures to new heights.

★ Exclusive strategies for profiting from the ever-expanding digital real estate market.

★ A comprehensive roadmap for navigating the complexities of virtual property wholesaling with confidence and expertise.

★ The opportunity to stay ahead of the curve and position yourself as a trailblazer in the evolving landscape of real estate investment.

Don't miss the chance to revolutionize your approach to real estate wholesaling and embark on a transformative journey into the realm of virtual properties. **"Virtual Real Estate Gold"** is your gateway to unlocking unparalleled success in the digital age. **Join me let's discover the deep secrets of real estate in the Digital Age**

Chapter 1

How a novice investor get started in the world of digital real estate

Because of the internet, our ways of living, working, and investing have all changed significantly. The rise of digital real estate gives investors new opportunities as well as new risks, making it one of the most significant shifts. The term **"digital real estate"** refers to the ownership of online assets, such as domain names, social media pages, websites, and virtual real estate, as well as the investment in these assets. Through the course of this book, we will investigate what digital real estate is, how it functions, as well as the opportunities and challenges that it presents to investors.

Process of managing digital properties

Investment in traditional real estate and investment in digital real estate both function in comparable ways. The acquisition, lease, and sale of virtual assets, such as social media accounts, websites, domain names, and virtual real estate, are all included in this process. The digital properties that may be found in online games and platforms such as **Second Life, Decentraland,** and The **Sandbox** are referred to as virtual real estate on the internet.Entrepreneurs who invest in digital real estate have several opportunities to generate income from their investments. These opportunities include **advertising, affiliate marketing, and the sale of products and services.** Numerous factors, including website traffic, domain authority, social media followers, and virtual land demand, impact the value of digital assets.

<u>Is Investing in Digital Real Estate Legit and Profitable?</u>

Although it has hazards and obstacles, investing in digital real estate is a decent concept. Digital assets have the potential to increase over time and generate high returns on investment, much like traditional real estate. On the other hand, investing in digital real estate needs skills in social media management, website design, and online marketing.It may be challenging to navigate the world of digital real estate, especially for **newbies**. Investing in meaningful and relevant digital assets, receiving expert help, and completing significant market and property research are some tips for buyers, sellers, and investors. Investors need to be updated on the most current developments and breakthroughs in the digital real estate business.Investing in profitable websites, acquiring and selling domain names, purchasing virtual land and residences, and engaging in online companies are just a few of the numerous opportunities for making investments in digital real estate. Investors have to pick alternatives depending on their financial goals, areas of expertise, and interests.

How Can I Invest in Digital Real Estate and Earn Money?

The market for digital real estate is rising swiftly, presenting investors with new possibilities for profit. A range of digital assets, including websites and virtual land, are now reachable for investment due to the advent of the internet and new technologies. There are various options for producing cash from digital real estate. Revenue from advertising is one of the most regularly employed tactics. _**By leveraging services like Google AdSense, MediaVine, and AdThrive, website owners may generate money by placing adverts on their websites.**_ In addition, individuals could gain cash using affiliate marketing, in which they get paid a commission for recommending items or services. Selling products or services online is another technique to benefit from digital real estate. With e-commerce platforms like Amazon, Etsy, and Shopify, anyone can sell things to people all over the world. Virtual land and properties in online games and platforms may be sold by virtual real estate investors to earn cash.

Creating Profitable Websites and Blogs

One of the easiest approaches to investing in digital real estate is to develop a lucrative website or blog. Your website may be made lucrative by delivering content that generates a lot of visitors via sponsorships, affiliate marketing, and advertising. To produce financial advantages, you may also acquire an already-established website or blog and grow it.Creating successful websites and blogs is one of the most well-liked strategies for investing in digital real estate. This is because learning it may be extremely easy and have a huge potential return on investment. You may establish a website or blog in your own time with minimal upfront investment. When you build a blog or website that has a big audience, you may sell it for more money than you initially paid, generating a substantial profit.Additionally, blogs and websites may generate passive money via sponsored content, affiliate marketing, and advertising, among other techniques. You may receive a continuous income without actively maintaining a blog or website by monetizing it. For people wanting a passive income stream, this makes it a viable investment alternative. Creating websites and blogs also offers the advantage of long-term growth potential. A blog or website's valuation could grow dramatically if it has a committed following. Because of this, potential buyers may view it to be a desired asset and be willing to pay more for a website that already has a significant following. Furthermore, making blogs and websites may be a gratifying creative undertaking. It helps individuals to share their views and interests in a way that resonates with their audience. Additionally, it may give opportunities for networking, cooperation, and personal growth.

Marketing Digital Goods

Investing in digital real estate may also be done by selling digital items like software, eBooks, and online courses. By generating helpful and unique digital items, you may develop a committed consumer base and generate money from your offers. To extend your consumer base and enhance earnings, you may also offer your items on websites like Etsy or Amazon.com.

Letting Go of Digital Property

Digital real estate may be leased out in the same manner as physical real estate. This entails leasing virtual land in virtual worlds, selling digital ad space, and renting out website space. You may benefit from any financial advantages in addition to a continuous income flow by renting out your digital real estate.

Switching NFTs and Domain Names

In the area of digital real estate, flipping non-fungible tokens (NFTs) and domain names is another lucrative enterprise. You may gain by acquiring and selling NFTs and domain names at the proper periods. To earn a profit, however, you must be cautious and know what you are doing as this may be harmful. In the area of digital real estate, non-fungible tokens, or NFTs, offer an alternative income source.Purchasing a domain name at a bargain and then reselling it for a profit is known as "flipping" domain names. Due to the rising tendency of organizations striving to establish a strong online presence, this method has gained favor in recent years. Finding domain names that are in high demand and that companies can quickly brand is the key to successful domain flipping. The most desirable domain names are frequently those with an a.com extension, are short, and are memorable. NFTs are scarce and valuable because they are one-of-a-kind digital assets that are validated on a blockchain and cannot be replicated. They may be tweets, movies, music, or even digital artwork. NFTs are gaining in popularity as more people and corporations embrace digital ownership. The most expensive NFT ever sold was a digital work of art developed by Beeple that earned an incredible $69 million at a Christie's auction in March 2021. While some investors utilize NFTs as a method of monetizing their digital works, others acquire and hold them in expectation of future value development. To monetize their work and reward their most loyal followers, musicians may, for instance, develop NFTs of their songs and sell them to supporters.Because the value of these assets could change and be unexpected, investing in NFTs might be perilous. Nonetheless, NFTs may be a fascinating and profitable approach to investing in digital real estate for those who are intrigued by the prospective rewards.

Purchasing Cryptocurrency

One frequent technique for investing in digital real estate is via cryptocurrency. Cryptocurrencies are decentralized digital money that function without the intervention of a central bank. Examples of these include Bitcoin, Ethereum, and Litecoin.Cryptocurrencies are constructed on advanced algorithms and encryption, in contrast to traditional currencies, which are backed by promises from the government.The possibility for bigger returns than traditional investments is one of the reasons that drives investors to cryptocurrency investing.For instance, Bitcoin's value climbed in 2021 from $29,374.15 on January 1 to $46,306.45 on December 31. It twice exceeded the $60,000 level, most notably on November 10, when it set its all-time high of $68,789.63.It's vital to realize, however,that cryptocurrencies may also be highly volatile, with huge swings in value happening fast. As of 2 March 2023, the price of Bitcoin (BTC) has climbed dramatically, hitting over $20,000 and gaining nearly 40% since the start of the year. This gain in value has corresponded with the US Federal Reserve's (Fed) expected slowdown in interest rate hikes. You must register for an account with a cryptocurrency exchange to invest in cryptocurrencies. You may buy and sell them using fiat money or other cryptocurrencies on these exchanges. Exchanges for cryptocurrencies that are well-known include **Binance, Kraken, and Coinbase.** Investing in cryptocurrencies via a mutual fund or exchange-traded fund (ETF) is an additional way. By enabling you to invest in a diversified portfolio of cryptocurrencies, these funds help you decrease the risk associated with owning just one single currency.It is vital to realize that investing in cryptocurrencies includes hazards, such as the chance of fraud and hacking. Before making any cryptocurrency investments,you should always undertake comprehensive research and only spend money that you can afford to lose. Keeping updated on the most current changes in Bitcoin news and trends is also vital, as it may considerably impact the return on your investment.

Digital Property in the Metaverse

The notion of virtual real estate in the metaverse has gained a lot of attention and funding in recent years. The metaverse is an online environment where users may participate in virtual reality interactions with one another and their surroundings. Users in this digital world may possess virtual assets that they may use for socializing, gaming, and economic transactions, among other activities.One of the most well-liked metaverse markets for virtual estate investing is Decentraland. Users may buy and possess "LAND," a virtual space that they can utilize to build, create, and generate money off of. Investors may gain by selling their property or by converting it into a valuable asset and producing money from it, like an internet store or amusement park.Another metaverse platform that has gained a lot of attention is Sandbox, where users may acquire virtual property and transform it into a variety of leisure facilities, such as game rooms, museums, and music halls. Celebrities and venture capitalists have made big investments on the site, and several high-profile partnerships have been uncovered.Compared to conventional real estate, investing in virtual real estate in the metaverse offers various advantages. Compared to traditional real estate, the admission fee is significantly less, and there is less red tape in the regulatory procedure. Furthermore, compared to genuine assets, virtual properties may be produced and sold substantially more rapidly, delivering larger returns on investment. Similar to traditional real estate, the metaverse's virtual real estate is valued depending on supply and demand. The demand for virtual dwellings will increase as more individuals join the metaverse, which will enhance the value of virtual real estate. With any investment, there are pitfalls, however, including the chance for the metaverse platform to lose attractiveness or fail to develop momentum.

Real Estate Using Tokens

The process of establishing digital tokens that stand in for ownership or investment in real estate is known as **"tokenized real estate."** These tokens are commonly developed on blockchains, which allow a transparent and secure mechanism of transferring and monitoring token ownership.By tokenizing real estate, investors may purchase and hold a fraction of a property without having to buy the entire thing or face the traditional difficulties and expenditures associated with real estate ownership. This may open up the real estate market to a bigger set of investors, including those who would not have the money to purchase a property completely.When corporations and platforms study the notion of tokenized real estate, they generally acquire properties and then partition ownership into digital tokens that investors can buy and maintain. Investors may acquire and sell a share of the property by exchanging these tokens on internet exchanges or platforms. **RealT** is one instance of a platform that delivers tokenized real estate investments. RealT enables investors to acquire digital tokens that are ownership equivalents of real estate based in the US. The platform makes use of blockchain technology to ensure secure and transparent ownership, and investors may obtain rewards frequently based on how much the property rents for. *The benefits of digital real estate include cost savings, ease, and efficiency.* Among the numerous benefits of investing in digital real estate are decreased transaction costs, greater flexibility, and easier access to a global market. You may invest in digital real estate with any amount of money, at any time, and from any place. By managing their properties from any place in the world, investors may save money on labor, utilities, and rent.

Additionally, they may automate time efficiency-saving activities like inventory management, customer assistance, and online payments.We are witnessing a revolution in real estate deals because of blockchain technology. Blockchain is a decentralized digital record that removes the need for intermediaries like banks or lawyers and allows secure and transparent transactions. There are various benefits to blockchain technology,including decreased costs, speedier transaction times, and increased security and transparency.

Digital Real Estate's Obstacles and Restrictions: Handling Access, Equity, and Trust Issues

Although there are various benefits to digital real estate, there are negatives as well that must be taken into mind. Ensuring equal access to digital real estate potential is a fundamental challenge. There may be a digital divide in the real estate market as a consequence of not everyone having access to the resources or technology necessary to invest in digital real estate.Establishing credibility in transactions using digital real estate is another problem. These include the danger of cyberattacks, fraud, and hacking in addition to the lack of monitoring and oversight. It is necessary to make a comprehensive investigation and appreciate the related hazards before investing in digital real estate.Policymakers and industry leaders need to unite to eliminate these hurdles and ensure that everyone, regardless of socioeconomic background, may benefit from digital real estate potential. One method to achieve this would be to give education and information to folks so they can learn about investing in and utilizing digital real estate. It may also entail putting regulations and procedures into place to assure the security and safety of transactions involving digital real estate.

In summary, the rise of digital real estate is transforming the real estate industry and opening up new avenues for buyers, sellers, and investors alike. Virtual property tours and blockchain technology are just two of the various benefits that digital real estate delivers, coupled with cost savings and simplicity. But technology also carries with it concerns like trust, equity, and accessibility that must be overcome. Leaders in the industry and policymakers can ensure that investment in digital real estate is safe and open to everyone by collaborating.

Accepting the Difficulties and Possibilities of the Digital Age: A Whole-System Approach to Digital Prominence

It is vital to recognize and solve the special issues offered by the virtual workplace as it continues to transform the face of work and collaboration. The key to effectively managing this always-shifting virtual terrain is adopting powerful methods that are tailored to the fluidity of digital interactions. Making advantage of the numerous tools available for collaboration and communication is a vital element of this journey. These technologies constitute the lifeblood of the virtual world, assuring that effective and efficient collaboration is still feasible even in the face of physical distances. However, how these technologies are utilized to foster a sense of community is just as essential as the actual tools themselves. For remote team members, who typically cope with the obstacles of isolation and distance, this is particularly vital. The core of a successful virtual team is a fluid workflow and good morale, which can only be preserved by developing this sense of community.Maintaining true links that pierce across digital barriers is the key to staying engaged and connected with virtual colleagues. Here's where the ability of virtual communication becomes crucial; it calls for a comprehensive plan to make sure that each team member feels connected, heard, and valued.It is now necessary, not discretionary, to employ technology to properly integrate real and virtual worlds. Ensuring that the limits of remote work locations do not hamper productivity and success is dependent upon this integration. Furthermore, it is crucial to establish a safe and secure environment for virtual meetings and interactions in a world where data is king. Any virtual interaction approach should emphasize data and privacy protection.But the journey doesn't end here. Staying ahead of the competition in the competitive climate involves keeping up to speed with the newest breakthroughs and trends in virtual technology. Successful virtual teams and organizations are distinguished by their constant learning and adaptation. The process of growing acclimated to the new virtual world demands endurance, practice, and an open mind. It's about learning from every experience, accepting change, and trying new instruments and approaches. The trick to excelling in the virtual world is this adaptability.

Ultimately, it's vital to take a break from the bustle of virtual exchanges and re-establish a connection with the actual world. A good work-life balance entails taking breaks, spending time in nature, and setting aside time for self-recharge. This all-encompassing method makes sure that even as we prosper in the virtual world, we never forget the simple joys and healing qualities that come from being in nature.To sum up, effectively navigating the virtual world demands a multimodal strategy that embraces technology, develops community, provides security, and encourages steady growth and stability. These recommendations will help us move ahead in this digital era and build a more pleasant, productive, and connected virtual experience.

The Top 14 Software Tools for Real Estate Wholesaling to Drive Your Business in 2024

The greatest real estate wholesaling software tools and features will be explored in this section and education guide for real estate wholesalers.To assist you in determining whether it makes sense for you to incorporate a given tool in your investment procedures, we also offer some insight into how most software vendors price each product.You'll know precisely the software you need to expand your real estate firm by the time you're done reading.Are you prepared to have a lucrative software roadmap?Now let's get underway!

First, the top lead-generating tools are:

1. Program for Acquiring Motivated Seller Leads

A dart board with three darts signifying a lead generation in the bull's eyeTo put it simply, wholesaling depends on your skill to discover owners who are willing to sell quickly.The term **"quickly"** is key in this circumstance, and intelligent wholesalers employ real estate wholesaling software to shorten the amount of time required to discover such owners.Rather than providing promotional materials to every citizen in a given location, they first employ the program to discover simply those people who fulfill preset motivation and property criteria.They may, for instance, pick a list of just high equity, absentee, or vacant owners.Purchasing lists of persons who satisfy your wholesale needs provides your organization an edge and helps it to develop much more swiftly.Features like these are featured in the leading software for producing real estate leads more rapidly.

Capability to stack multiple lead types utilizing advanced list-stacking gives free leads that have previously been traced down to gather the contact data of property owners. The greatest software provides free leads that are already tracked so you can start marketing straight away. (99% of software that purports to provide you free leads doesn't give you any contact information and needs you to still skip trace them, so they are not free. It is linked with a multi-channel Customer Relationship Management (CRM) system to offer quick communication. Certain software sellers promise that their monthly subscription offers an unending supply of free leads. They cannot be promptly marketed to and do not supply contact information, so they are not leads. Compare simple leads with contact information and their cost per lead.Unqualified leads with contact data normally cost $0.20 per lead, however, more might be paid for some difficult-to-find lead kinds. Software that sells leads is available for $0 to $295 a month, depending on the additional services supplied.A part of free motivated seller leads that have already been skip traced is included with

REI/kit wholesaling software solutions, enabling you to begin marketing without having to initially pay for skip tracing. After getting leads via different sources, such as buying lead lists, you may begin advertising them.

2. Software for Direct Mail Marketing

Direct mail is still beneficial for advertising your firm to motivated salespeople as it reaches your lead immediately where they are.A large audience is attracted to direct mail since it has good deliverability rates and delivers postcards that recipients can cling to until they're ready to sell.

Features of direct mail software consist of:

- ★ Ready-made postcard designs for rapid direct mail campaigns

- ★ Alternatives for personalization, such as logo

- ★ There are several sizes and speeds available.

★ Possibility of mailing numerous contacts at once with direct mail postcards

★ Sending multi-weekly postcard drip campaigns

★ Mailing service integration with applications for speedier mailing

★ Tracking mail events

Depending on the number of mailings you send, the median monthly membership price for businesses that offer direct mail sends is $125. The monthly membership price grows with the volume of mail you send.The least-priced postcard has an average unit cost of $0.875,The lowest size Direct Mail postcards offered from REI/kit on the most popular plan cost $0.686.

3. SMS Text Messaging Software for Real Estate

With read and reply rates reaching 95% and higher, SMS text marketing is highly successful.For real estate wholesalers wishing to strike up a quick talk, SMS is excellent.The following are the major features of SMS marketing software:

Send a flood of text messages to both buyers and sellers.

★ drip campaigns with many texts

★ pre-made templates for SMS

★ Get SMS messages utilizing two-way messaging.

★ integrated with a CRM to capture discussions

AI makes it possible to acquire the greatest response rates.Depending on the services and integrations you require, the fees could vary dramatically.For instance, you may pay for an SMS-sending platform that offers simply the sending capability and may not have a monthly subscription.This is not a good option for most marketers unless you are highly computer-informed, as it won't have the tools required to conduct successful campaigns.Software that supports SMS transmission has an average monthly membership fee of $125, with an average cost per message of $0.04.The most popular plan's REI/kit cost is $104 for a membership, with $0.03 per text message.

4. Software for Ringless Voicemail (RVM)

Software that automates voicemail leads is a more effective approach to creating real estate leads via cold calling.Without ringing the lead's phone, a ringless voicemail drop gently sends your recorded message to their voicemail box.Ringless voicemail is a wonderful alternative if you've ever wanted your message to be heard by thousands of people to make that initial contact and obtain follow-up calls.

<u>Features of the RVM software consist of:</u>

★ **Bringing in your voicemails**

★ **Possibility of blasting voicemails**

★ **Weekly drip campaigns from RVM**

Since ringless voicemail software isn't supplied by many carriers, monthly membership prices are frequently higher, averaging $200.Depending on how many you send, the normal cost of each RVM fluctuates, but you should budget roughly $0.10 for each message.

5. Software for Email Marketing

Email is a low-risk, low-cost marketing strategy that's a terrific place to start when presenting your brand and solution proposition to sellers who are interested in knowing more.The following are the top features of email marketing software:

★ Emails are delivered automatically to sellers who fill up a website contact form

★ Content placeholders can cut down on tiresome entries, such as first name or property address

★ makes use of back-end technology and best practices to boost deliverability

The send volume or the amount of contacts frequently influences the email marketing software membership prices.Because of this, pricing may vary substantially, from free to hundreds of dollars each month, with the volume of emails sent also having a considerable influence on unit costs per email.

6. Phone System for Following Up and Cold Calling

Reaching out to sellers via cold calling is a fantastic tactic, but there's a creative way to accomplish it.

You and your organization are safeguarded when you use a virtual phone number instead of your real number.Obtaining virtual numbers—also referred to as burner or throw-away numbers—has numerous additional advantages.For each campaign you develop, you may set up a phone number to measure the success of responses to that particular campaign. Additionally, you have the ability to set a particular quantity for each seller's location. You quickly become more familiar and relevant if you select an area code that matches the recipients.To keep a check on your virtual assistants' or team members' performance, you may also supply them with phone numbers.

<u>Features of virtual phone numbers include:</u>

- ★ Able to identify select numbers for RVM, SMS marketing, and cold calling
- ★ There are various phone numbers available.
- ★ Give team members numbers to use for receiving and outgoing calls.
- ★ A contact is instantly established in the CRM when a call comes in.
- ★ Option to send calls to voicemail or route them to one or more recipients
- ★ Available for transcription and recording
- ★ Web phone for virtual assistants working overseas

Software that enables you to make outgoing calls frequently includes a monthly subscription charge of $100. such as a conventional phone plan, such software may feature some metered-use items, such as a bundle of included minutes.

Typical additional charges consist of:

Phone numbers, including toll-free numbers, cost an additional

Talk time is frequently compensated in minutes, rounded up.

Conversation recording is also priced on a per-minute basis.

7. Multi-Platform Advertising Initiatives

The top marketing software for real estate wholesalers helps you to blend approaches and develop unique multi-channel campaigns as we just mentioned.**Omni-channel marketing**, another term for multi-channel marketing, offers various benefits. These benefits include enhanced outreach to connections, inconspicuous marketing for wholesalers, and an effective communication system.

The following are the major features of multi-channel marketing software:

★ Ready-to-use multi-day campaigns

★ campaigns targeted at various kinds of interested suppliers

★ Create your campaigns with any combination of Send out campaign updates gradually or all at once.

★ creation of a task upon receipt of a response

This program has a monthly membership charge that varies from $65 to $300. Instead of comparing pricing, you should compare the quantity of marketing channels that are enabled.A CRM will keep you focused and on target, while multi-channel scalability offers the potential to grow your lead creation.

8. Top CRM (Customer Relationship Management) Software for Real Estate

All of your contacts for real estate business are consolidated in CRM software.An online CRM is particularly handy if you have been taking notes, scanning documents, or employing Post-its. You may engage with and, most importantly, follow up with your leads using the CRM. Ultimately, a complete real estate CRM created with real estate wholesalers in mind will expedite the workflow of contact management and arrange activities.

<u>Features of CRM databases include:</u>

Ability to engage with your motivated seller prospects and other contacts via phone, email, text messaging, and direct mail immediately from within the CRM

- ★ **View a history of your activities**
- ★ **Launch a marketing automation campaign utilizing contacts.**
- ★ **Create tasks automatically.**
- ★ **Assign team members to tasks.**
- ★ **You may easily skip-trace a contact in the CRM.**

Data gathering:

Lead paperwork for seller properties and property details

integrated with online forms

Using Zapier, linked with external systems

Advanced filtering and data management:

Divide contacts such as buyers, sellers, and other types.

Put labels on it

Establish status

Upload and store documents and photos.

Bring in a lead list from a file.

A mapping tool is available for swiftly allocating data columns.To gain additional contact information, skip trace imported leads.The majority of online CRMs employ a subscription payment structure depending on the amount of contacts saved.This sum may be as low as free or as much as hundreds of dollars every month.

9. Tools for Skip Tracing

Provided to real estate wholesalers, contact data are crucial.Without a way to sell to them, a list of property owners' names and addresses is meaningless.By bridging the gap, skip tracing services allow investors to acquire the owners' postal addresses, phone numbers, or email addresses.

Among the top skip-tracing programs are:

Fast results from in-house or on-platform processing as opposed to data orders that take a considerable time to complete and necessitate a separate service. Data was quickly recovered as opposed to having to be exported and imported from various applications.

Pricing normally runs from $0.12 to $0.15 per contact, depending on whether or not Do-Not-Call lookups are included.The finest software does not impose a minimum order quantity on skip trace requests.After discovering the phone numbers, it also completes the vital Do Not Call registration.

10. Lead-generating websites presented on a mobile phone, tablet, and laptop

Websites for real estate wholesalers aid three vital parts of managing a reputable company: lead generation, brand awareness, and conveying a polished image to sellers and other investors.

<u>Features of the website builder for real estate wholesalers include:</u>

- ★ **Website templates with excellent conversion rates created exclusively for investors and wholesalers**
- ★ **Simple to create**

- ★ Possibility of attaching a domain name to the website
- ★ involves hosting
- ★ Personalization includes a digital phone number, images, and a corporate insignia
- ★ Google search engine optimized
- ★ Personalized URL to market the website to suppliers using Facebook, Google, or Instagram advertisements
- ★ Including connections to Google Ads, Facebook Retargeting Pixel, and Google Search Console
- ★ pulls in sellers who wish to put in their data for a cash offer.
- ★ brings in cash buyers who offer their specifications for a real estate transaction.
- ★ responsive on mobile
- ★ A CRM is automatically supplied leads from lead capture.

It also have the Possibility of displaying property under contract to prospective cash buyers. Average Cost—-$40–$65 per month. You'll need data and information to assess the properties once those transactions start rolling in.

11. Deal Analysis for Real Estate Investors

To add value to a transaction, wholesalers, investors, and other real estate professionals need to be aware of all the nuances surrounding a real estate investment opportunity.For a lucrative pipeline of deals, the best real estate wholesaling software also ought to have a deal analysis platform.Lenders, property flippers, and customers will all have access to complete financials and comparisons owing to the software.

Features of the top investment analysis software include:

★ **Examine wholesale transaction**

★ **Run precise comparisons**

★ Determine the ARV.

★ Tool for modifying comps to concentrate on value

★ Calculate the cost of rehab.

★ Give the 70% rule calculations.

★ Examine additional property categories

★ PR potential, multi-family cash flow analysis, and rents

★ Estimate of property rehabilitation

★ Analysis of exit alternatives for different real estate investment types

★ Property information

★ Property records and information, including property value, tax rolls, and assessments

★ Top-notch comparisons from public data sources

The monthly cost of software that merely delivers analysis is $50.

12. Real estate investment and wholesaling marketing reports

You must not only assess the deal but also build a process to convey your findings to the essential stakeholders in the transaction.Creating property reports for dissemination to lenders, cash buyers, and other real estate investors should be a straightforward operation for software built for wholesaling real estate.

<u>Features include</u>

- The development of transaction reports for cash purchasers, lenders, and private money should be incorporated.
- Show the repair estimate and transaction circumstances, and present comparisons and ARV.
- The capacity to switch sensitive information on and off
- the ability to give reports in different formats

A single report should cost you anywhere from $5 to several hundred dollars.

13. Consolidations

When employing real estate wholesaling software or other tools in their company, wholesalers should verify that they can integrate them with other systems.Zapier is a renowned integration partner that simplifies the construction of connections between apps.These interfaces may be used, for instance, to transmit data immediately into a CRM from forms on other websites.Certain real estate wholesale software involves upgrading to a premium plan or levies an add-on price of $25–$35 for a membership.

14. The real estate investment Team Access

You are the main hurdle to your ability to grow your company, and the most successful business owners recognize that establishing teams is crucial to increasing their companies.Teams may be assisted by the greatest software for real estate wholesaling. Teams of investors and real estate wholesalers must be able to work on the same projects, leads, CRM, and other business-related duties.This is true for both purchases and sales or both combined.

<u>Features of the team include:</u>

The software's capacity to enable partners and other real estate investors to use it

Collaborate with cold call teams, marketers, web designers, virtual assistants, and other professionals.

limited views or permission-based access to particular features in your account.

It is usual to pay each team member roughly $20 for each seat.

Using Marketing Automation Tools to Scale

Automation is vital for developing your business, and we've explained the type of software you'll need to fulfill your aims as effectively as possible.The most successful approach to scaling up the search for highly motivated sellers is automation.Marketing tactics employed in the past to discover wholesale properties included bandit signs, paper marketing pamphlets, driving for payment, and letter writing.

These strategies involve looking at each property separately and then getting in contact with the owners to determine their degree of enthusiasm.But there is one problem that unifies them all: **size.**To reach thousands of consumers at once, you may also need to initiate automated campaigns that deliver postcards, SMS, ringless voicemail, or email marketing to achieve scalability.You may also up to five times your transaction flow and improve your marketing reach by employing five channels for each lead.It could be hard and time-consuming to launch marketing campaigns for each lead employing various software packages for each marketing channel. The key to success is real estate wholesale software that includes each of these tactics and simplifies the process.

Important Learning

A software system that combines marketing, follow-up, and transaction analysis skills is crucial if you want to expand your real estate wholesale firm more rapidly and accomplish more deals.The top 14 real estate wholesaling tools and features that you should include in your real estate wholesaling systems are discussed above. When integrated successfully, they may help you enhance lead generation by automating repetitive activities, lowering lead nurturing efforts, and efficiently managing lead communication to clinch more business.With confidence, you should now be able to pick the features and tools your real estate wholesaling software system requires to meet all of your company's goals.

Digital-Age Real Estate Important Trends to Keep an Eye on in 2024

Over the previous 10 years, the real estate technology startup market has risen by 300%, leveraging technology to solve some of the industry's most critical concerns. The coronavirus's quick spread has sped the digital transformation of the real estate business as corporations have had to immediately adapt.Technology in real estate looks to have a very bright future. Over eighty percent of real estate organizations desire to incorporate new technologies into their regular business practices. Given that investment activity reached $9.7 billion in the first half of the previous year, it is not a surprise that it is continuing to expand. Using the relevant tech trends at the appropriate moment is important to developing a successful real estate IT organization. **JatApp** has been aiding real estate businesses with their digital transformation for the past six years. We have utilized our expertise and experience to tell you about the important business trends of the digital era in this book.. Let's get started right now.In the acquiring, financing, and selling of properties, artificial intelligence (AI) and machine learning (ML) These days, a lot of real estate organizations employ machine learning and artificial intelligence to make hard judgments. Compared to humans, they can conduct cognitively demanding tasks like reasoning and self-correction considerably more swiftly because of AI-powered technology. In the meantime, firms may make reliable projections utilizing machine learning and available data. The extensive application of AI and

ML is what fuels the real estate technology business, or PropTech. These days, there is active employment of these technologies in all parts of financing, acquiring, and selling real estate.

Purchasing a house

The National Association of Realtors says that 97% of buyers start their home searches online. Users may browse through hundreds of ads on real estate marketplaces to identify homes that meet their specifications. Here, an ML tool's potential to swiftly discover the elements that matter to prospective homeowners and make advice is useful. For instance, **Homes.com,** a digital real estate marketplace, employs machine learning algorithms to ensure a tailored housing search.

This is how it functions

Home purchasers may submit photographs of their dream homes or the homes across the street from them that they've always liked on Instagram or

Pinterest, and the site will show listings for homes with identical characteristics and aesthetics. AI has also increased the efficiency of the home-buying process for real estate agents. Agents may utilize AI to predict which residences are more likely to sell so they may approach homeowners first, saving time and energy compared to knocking on hundreds of homes. The computer checks facts about the property, such as the length of time the owner has resided there, neighborhood housing prices, and the date of the previous sale. Compass provides proof that artificial intelligence (AI) may enhance a broker's chances of receiving a property listing by as much as 94%. With the usage of the company's platform, agents may more accurately target house sellers by establishing the price of the property.

The possibility of a property sale as forecasted by AI Compass

Professional house appraisers used to be responsible for determining the worth of residences up for sale. These days, artificial intelligence (AI) can appraise the value of a home remotely using photos of the interior and a neural network that detects distinct features of the property that determine the pricing.

Let's employ the well-known home-selling portal HouseCanary as an example to aid you acquire an understanding. A complete 20-page home evaluation report that describes the elements that lead to the ultimate price is delivered to sellers by AI. Additionally, sellers may employ the HouseCanary service for just $59 instead of having to pay up to $900 for standard property evaluations. The firm is leveraging AI technology to upend traditional evaluation techniques in terms of competitive price and speed.

House Loans

The mortgage process may now be streamlined, from picking the optimal loan type to locating investors, owing to improvements in AI technology. These days, borrowers may see how much money they are losing yearly and monthly in a matter of seconds.The mortgage lender LoanSnap employs artificial intelligence (AI) to assess the borrower's financial information, filter through thousands of possible loans, identify the best one, and calculate the best ways of debt payback. AI supports customers in making challenging mortgage-related decisions, resulting in future financial savings.

Loan matching with LoanSnap AI-powered loan matching using LoanSnap

There has been a decline in demand for on-location visits during the global outbreak, with 90% of sellers agreeing to limit visits to their homes. After conversing with each property seller, most buyers no longer require a house tour owing to virtual reality. Clients may view the property they admire from the comfort of their couch with virtual home tours. With the help of this technology, buyers may virtually tour the property as if they were there in person. Virtual room views enable purchasers to spin around, check the floor and ceiling, and see numerous stories. Even properties that are currently under construction may be digitally accessed by people as if they were already done. To give customers an immersive 3D experience, Matterport, a significant participant in the virtual tour sector, combines innovative machine vision technology and deep learning algorithms. Compared to 2D photographs of properties, customers report that the company's virtual tours enhance interest by 300%. Virtual tours, according to 74% of Matterport brokers, have boosted their number of property listings.

Intelligent Structures

Often referred to as intelligent buildings or smart buildings, these structures make use of **Internet of Things (IoT)** sensors to collect data on numerous building-related subjects. This data is then examined and utilized to enhance building operations while also being more environmentally friendly. Aside from that, technology may help to better the comfort, safety, and productivity of building residents. With its IoT power bank sharing stations, a French startup that JatApp works with supports companies and educational institutions in adopting building intelligence. Employees may function without being restricted to their office workstations by renting charging bases and portable power banks owing to this option. The client obtained support from JatApp in designing the software that connects the base and power banks.

IoT-capable power supply platform for rentals

Automation in all elements of property management Property managers may simply automate several boring duties. Landlords may now receive alerts when applications, credit reports, and criminal records are submitted via auto-tenant screening. Additionally, rent payments may be made online by landlords and tenants may receive reminders via technology when it's time to pay. In a similar vein, automation software warns landlords, tenants, and service providers of approaching events and maintenance needs. Based on our experience, JatApp created a mobile application and notification microservice for Cunio, a property management platform, and its German clients. With the aid of the digital solution, controlling every part of rental real estate is feasible, from screening new renters and collecting rent to publishing notifications and reacting to maintenance requests. Through the technology, service providers and homeowners may receive numerous notifications on their mobile phones and keep in continual touch.

Adapting communication styles

Technology is affecting how people seek to share and receive information. To fulfill the expectations of their consumers for quicker, easier, and more efficient communication, real estate businesses are being driven to develop new real estate digital strategies. Let's speak about the widespread communication preferences of today and how real estate technology enterprises are adjusting to satisfy these demands.

Frequent contact

Customers want responses to their concerns these days, whenever it's convenient for them. 24/7 customer service is offered by chatbots, but, if a human advisor is required, a person will be presented. Eighty percent of routinely asked inquiries may be addressed by chatbots.Chatbots are actively employed by real estate technology investing platforms, such as Crowdstreet, to aid investors in better understanding their investment possibilities and enabling them to make more intelligent selections. By assigning a virtual assistant to solve investor-specific concerns, the real estate site cuts service costs and saves time.

Quick reactions

Establishing a successful business-client relationship entails being able to react to them immediately. According to a Zillow Trends poll, 80% of customers view an agent's reaction to be vital. Customer relationship management (CRM), which helps agents organize and monitor talks with consumers and improve response times, is becoming increasingly popular among real estate organizations. The real estate marketplace Zillow designed a CRM system with auto-response features so that brokers could reply immediately away during their busiest period. Agents may modify their pitch to each client or group of consumers to ensure a more personalized approach. Additionally, the system informs brokers of incoming leads so they may reply as quickly as practical.

Sending texts

According to Forbes, the majority of today's workforce, millennials, prefer texting over phone calls. The bulk of smartphone users—nearly 90%—read incoming text messages fast. In addition, texting is generally quicker than phone calls, and users may interact asynchronously—that is, they may wait for a response while engaging themselves with other things. In property management, text messaging performs a range of roles, such as responding to queries about properties, arranging follow-ups, addressing maintenance requests, boosting workplace security, and so on. Recently, JatApp supported a facility management services provider in establishing a text-based mobile application that allows users to report near-miss occurrences at work.

Chapter 2

How To Develop A Complete Online Presence For Real Estate

A visually beautiful and well-built digital platform oozes exclusivity, reliability, and professionalism right instantly; the converse can drive away customers. Potential clients will remember your website and social media accounts favorably if you build a high-quality. These are some suggestions to take in mind when establishing your web presence, regardless of whether you work for a huge brokerage or alone as an agent.

Continue to communicate with the brand online.

Select a clean and elegant design that embodies the essence of both your present firm and luxury real estate. Include clean, beautiful typography, elegant color schemes, and high-quality pictures. In general, steer away from intricate patterns or flat, bright colors—trust your instincts.For a faultless user experience, make sure your website is mobile-friendly and straightforward to use. Consider providing property measurement, currency conversions, and language options for customers from various nations if you wish to develop into international markets. The trick is to adapt to the way your organization grows.

Display stunning pictures

There is a ton of visual competitiveness in the online realm. You have to put out effort to get people to notice you. Your website should incorporate high-quality photographs and videos to display the magnificence of your luxury mansions.Ensure that each property's traits, exquisite details, and beautiful views are represented in the images. Think about implementing virtual tours or 3D walkthroughs to create a more immersive element and present potential buyers with an up-close experience.

Give full information about the property.

Those who acquire luxury properties are frequently fairly meticulous when making purchases. Make sure every property on your platform has comprehensive and accurate information about it, including floor plans, amenities, geographical information, and adjacent attractions. Highlight the particular attributes and distinguishing aspects that make each property exceptional.

Add stuff from a blog or magazine.

Make your website a destination for new clients as well as present ones. Give particular attention to intriguing and instructive information concerning luxury real estate. give relevant and inspiring information for potential clients, or give links to it. Articles displaying stunning architectural designs, insider tips for organizing opulent parties, and interior design trends may all come under this category.Disseminating useful and motivating information boosts your brand as a trusted luxury real estate agent (or business) and confirms your expertise. Content has a long-term plan. You never know when a frequent reader or website visitor will become a buyer instead of simply a casual clicker. Recall that an engaging online presence acts as a vital digital manifestation of your organization and showcases the exceptional attributes your group represents. Additionally, it helps you to separate yourself apart from other brokerages and develop a unique character in a highly competitive sector.By returning to the basics, you may catapult your organization to new heights. Make a magnificent, well-thought-out space that helps your customers. You'll be amazed by the booming spring real estate market in Altos.A thriving real estate market is characterized by growing house prices, rising sales, and steadily rising inventory.

Seven Ways to Boost Your Real Estate Broker Online Presence

Your online presence serves as many potential consumers' initial impression of your real estate agency. You must utilize the internet's power correctly if you want to flourish in this digital era and separate yourself from the competition. To build their firm and interact with new customers, real estate agents in the current digital world must have a strong online presence. A solid online presence may considerably boost your chances of success as more and more potential consumers are utilizing the internet to hunt for properties and real estate services. These seven intelligent tips might help you, as a real estate broker, make the most of your online presence and develop your firm to new heights.

1. Invest in a Website That Is Easy to Use

Your real estate company's online showroom is your website. Make sure it is user-friendly, responsive, and professional. Since many people browse websites using smartphones and tablets, mobile optimization is vital. Add buttons for organizing consultations and contact forms, or other apparent calls to action. A successful user experience relies on clear design, rapid download speeds, and high-quality pictures.

2. Gain Expertise in Social Media

Utilize social media platforms' potential to develop a relationship with your audience. On well-known platforms like Facebook, Instagram, WhatsApp channels, and YouTube, build appealing profiles. Distribute eye-catching content, such as photographs of the property, videos, and instructive articles about the real estate sector. Interact with your followers by rapidly addressing their messages and comments. Relationships and trustworthiness are developed by meaningful and continuous participation.

3. Accept Video Marketing

Online video content has surged in popularity. Digital marketing is growing, and reels on Instagram and YouTube are the new norm. Make engaging videos featuring house tours, guides to the neighborhood, and real estate advice. Engage in real-time conversation with potential clients via live streaming and virtual open houses. Videos offer your company a human face and help you create a connection with your audience that will boost their faith in your expertise.

4. Search engine optimization (SEO)

Utilizing effective SEO tactics may considerably boost your website's visibility on search engines such as Google. To find out what potential clients are searching for, undertake keyword research and change your website's optimization suitably. By integrating location-specific keywords in your content, focus on local SEO. To boost your website's search engine ranking, supply fresh, relevant information often. Not only does well-written information attract readers, but it also improves your authority in the industry.

5. Make Use of Email Marketing

One of the strongest techniques to nurture leads and retain touch with consumers is still email marketing. Create an email list with potential sellers, buyers, and other real estate agents. Distribute newsletters periodically with market updates, new listings, tips on acquiring and selling a property, and other useful information. Tailor your emails to the particular needs and tastes of the individuals who will be receiving them. By sending out useful emails, you can position yourself as a real estate industry expert and guarantee that recipients remember you and your services.

6. Highlight Customer Testimonials

Testimonials and endorsements from delighted customers are excellent techniques for creating trust. Put these endorsements front and center on your website and social media platforms. Urge delighted consumers to publish reviews on platforms such as Google My Business. Testimonials affect the decisions of potential customers by functioning as social proof of your expertise and the level of your services.

7. Produce Educational Blog Posts

You may give in-depth information on the real estate market, investment potential, home care recommendations, and more by running an active blog on your website. Writing instructional blog articles promotes you as an authority in the industry and provides natural traffic to your website. Respond to regularly requested concerns and anxieties from potential clients to exhibit your expertise and help.

The world of digital is continually evolving. Keep up with the most current advances in internet marketing trends and technologies. Use analytics tools to check your website's and social media channels' performance frequently. To identify which tactics are most successful, monitor user behavior, engagement metrics, and conversion rates. Make modifications to your online presence in response to the data, emphasizing on the channels and techniques that generate the highest results.In conclusion, a varied approach is essential to optimize your online presence as a real estate broker. You can build a strong online presence that brings in new consumers, develops trust, and positions your real estate firm as a pioneer in the digital arena by putting these seven tips into effect. In the competitive world of online real estate, establish a lasting impression by being proactive, authentic, and client-focused.

Use These Professional Tips to Maximize Social Media for Your Wholesale Business

Wholesalers and B2B buyers have progressed beyond the classic brick-and-mortar and paper-and-pencil models in today's connected and digitally-driven world. Social networking, digital marketing, and B2B eCommerce have all been employed by them.In truth, a CMO survey suggests that B2B firms spend 8.5–10.3% of their sales on marketing, with digital marketing accounting for about 50%–55.6% of this total.Put simply, wholesalers are embracing the digital spotlight and adopting social media, in particular, to fully harness the great potential of these online platforms in this age of communication.You'll have a better knowledge of the basic methods for making the most of social media networks like LinkedIn and Twitter by the end of this section. Let's get started and study how to utilize social media efficiently for your wholesale firm.

Why does B2B marketing need to integrate social media?

Social media platforms have matured into useful tools that help organizations connect, engage, and grow. They are now more than merely platforms to post cat memes.These digital platforms enable B2B firms previously unheard-of opportunities to enhance their revenue, customers, and influence, including:

Building brand awareness: With an expected 4.41 billion users by 2025, distributors and wholesale brands may considerably boost their visibility and reach a larger audience by having a presence on social media platforms. These platforms also allow you a venue to effectively exhibit and sell your brand identity, which helps set you apart from the competitors.

Lead generation: Wholesalers may utilize social media to locate and attract new customers by employing specialized content and advertising.

Promotions: B2B marketers have access to several tools and marketing choices on social media platforms to promote new items and push brands to select demographics, including sponsored posts and targeted advertising.

Engagement: B2B organizations may boost customer trust and loyalty by actively connecting with their audience on social media. More proof is required. Studies suggest that 84% of C-level executives and 75% of B2B purchasers are impacted by social media when making decisions on what to purchase.

Market research: By keeping a watch on talks, comments, and interactions, wholesale organizations may acquire significant information about customer preferences and trends. They are therefore able to adapt their marketing strategy properly.In the end, social media provides various options for everything from expanding market reach and brand development to developing deep B2B relationships and raising brand recognition.

Five expert recommendations for leveraging social media for wholesale

Although it's not straightforward to produce interesting social media posts, doing it properly may have a huge influence on your wholesale business's success. Here are five expert ideas that may help you leverage social media, develop an online presence that works for your customers, and optimize return on investment.

1. Establish your objectives

Just as you wouldn't go on a stroll without a map and compass, you can't develop an online presence without first outlining your objectives on social media. They function as a reference for the aims that B2B enterprises have. Having clearly defined goals, improving brand awareness or contact with your wholesale brand, or generating leads are all vital for attaining quantifiable results. In the end, goals aid marketers in tailoring strategy, data, and content to better meet their business ambitions.If your aim is, for instance, to build brand awareness for your wholesale eco-friendly packaging organization, this goal may be accomplished by expanding your following to a target amount (e.g., obtaining 5,000 followers). To achieve this, you may publish a series of articles explaining techniques for minimizing your effect on the environment or addressing the benefits of eco-friendly items and the relevance of sustainability.Setting objectives may ultimately help you select which social networking sites will best help you attain them. While their B2B rivals might choose to focus on a more business-oriented network like LinkedIn, B2C firms could select more consumer-driven media, such as TikTok and Instagram.

2. Teach instead of selling.

For B2B buyers, social media networks give up-to-date information on industry news, trends, and innovative breakthroughs. Additionally, they are perfect for creating thought leadership. Therefore, wholesale enterprises must give intelligent information, expert counsel, and instructional content on social media platforms. For instance, if you are a wholesale distributor of bridal wear, you could make an infographic explaining how a prospective bride can select the ideal dress for their wedding, complete with illustrations or photos of gowns in various styles according to particular themes (such as modern chic, bohemian cool, or classic cut).Instead of focusing just on earning purchases, try offering your followers fascinating and valuable material that they can talk about, discuss, and connect with your brand.Keep in mind that you interact with individuals, not merely corporations. According to a LinkedIn poll, thinking leadership with "a more human, less formal tone of voice" was favored by 64% of corporate executives over thought leadership with "an even-toned, intellectual voice."

3. Interact with peers and followers.

The usage of social media is mutual. Engaging in frequent engagement with your fans on social media is one of the finest ways to utilize the possibilities these platforms offer your wholesale firm.You may, for example, react to messages and comments, answer requests about your products and services, or encourage followers to give their distinctive insights and experience on a particular issue (i.e., seek advice or views). By following these straightforward steps, you can show your customers how devoted you are, create open communication, enhance transparency, and develop stronger, more trustworthy connections.To boost your visibility, share knowledge, and build contacts with colleagues and prospective business partners, you may also join organizations (such as those discussing supply management) or follow sites and profiles regarding your field.

4. Highlight client testimonials

Like success stories, testimonials, or interviews, client anecdotes are a superb approach to humanize your brand, develop credibility and trust with your followers, connect with them on an emotional level, and illustrate the advantages of your products and services. Social proof may also be offered by client testimonials that emphasize their beneficial experiences using your goods and the challenges they were able to remedy. They may convince potential clients and aid them get over their reluctance, which may enhance lead generation.It's also a terrific technique to receive consumer input on your providing, which you can employ to continually increase your items and exhibit your concern for their viewpoints.

5. Make use of eye-catching images

Not surprisingly, a picture speaks a thousand words, especially on social media. To cut through the clutter on social media, over 75% of marketers employ visuals.Professional videos or images with clarity, sharpness, and high quality may make a great impact, look attractive, capture attention, and enhance conversion rates.Lastly, keeping the same brand colors, fonts, and messaging across all of your social media posts and sites is vital to retaining a united brand identity.

What else should I remember?

Social media platforms are more than mere tools; they are a thriving ecosystem where B2B enterprises and brands develop their clientele, tell their stories, and come to life. In a dynamic, ever-evolving environment, it's vital to consistently:Remain educated. Be informed of how social media algorithms are developing to make sure your posts are viewed by the people who matter.Measure and study the information. Utilize social media analytics to monitor how effective your posts are and change your content approach as required.Social media has the ability to alter your wholesale firm as 46.5% of B2B buyers worldwide prefer to contact suppliers on these platforms.B2B firms may fully leverage these platforms by keeping informed, responding to new algorithms, undertaking data analysis, and employing the expert guidance offered in this article. In the end, taking advantage of these platforms helps you to enhance exposure, build a relationship with your audience, and achieve major economic benefits.

11 Online Networking Strategies To Create Fruitful Connections

What are the greatest strategies to "meet" new people and build such ties in a post-pandemic culture when practically all of our networking is done online? Here are some of my finest virtual networking **suggestions:**

1. Determine your specialization

Most of the time, picking a specialized problem is a superb technique to start creating your brand, which is a critical initial step in the method of virtual networking. I started by focusing on the strategic performance management niche, but as time went on, I also looked at other developing issues like artificial intelligence.

2. Consider the larger picture

Look beyond your gig economy or existing work and strive to identify issues that will become more essential in the future years. You might later decide to branch out into one of those areas, or it could wind up becoming your expertise.

3. Take modest steps at the start

It's OK to start small by adding a little bit more material to the networks you are now actively using. Don't put pressure on yourself to develop a presence on every website at once.

4. Utilize your profiles to make a distinctive impression.

Make sure your profiles have a current image and erase any information you wouldn't want customers or employers to access.

5. Post content on the internet that displays your skills and identifies you as an authority in your field.

This may contain controversial comments on topical themes today, bits from lectures you've done in the past, instructional resources, and more.

6. Join social media networks for your industry. Develop a reputation in the group by engaging in posts, replying to requests, and spreading other members' stuff.

7. Participate in as many free virtual conferences and events as you can. Online forums, conferences, and seminars are an excellent method to meet people and are accessible every day.

8. Make an introduction. If you engage in virtual events, be sure to identify yourself in the chat box with your location, desired job title, and sort of clients (if you work as a freelancer).

9. Locate relevant folks to reach out to. Find people who are active on the internet, reach out to workers at businesses that interest you, or get in contact with past colleagues. When you want to develop a connection and you need to make a request, be succinct and explicit in what you ask for.

10. Don't be a pest, but do follow up. Feel free to follow up a few times if you don't hear back, but avoid pressing the individual into replying or annoying them with too many follow-ups.

11. Consider setting some time each week for social media networking. Although it doesn't need a full-time job, cultivating connections does involve effort, so set up some time on your schedule for these hobbies. If you do decide to utilize social media, you may want to impose a time limit on how much time you spend there as these sites can be

major time wasters.If you don't enjoy attending major conferences and in-person events, you may still create a strong network. With these recommendations, you may construct an invincible virtual network and progress your vocation more swiftly.Users may construct and share their chatbots utilizing the platforms Cici AI, ChitChop, and Coze. Fictional narratives and language are created by BagelBell and are subject to reader discretion. However, ByteDance did not design the huge language models that support them. Rather, the apps employ OpenAI's GPT technology, which can be accessible via a Microsoft Azure license, according to Jodi Seth, a representative for ByteDance. ByteDance, whose ownership is being exposed here for the first time, is not listed on the websites of the new services or in their terms of service. In charge of three of them is Spring (SG) Pte. While ChitChop and Cici are largely entertainment-focused, delivering bots based on love interests and imaginary characters, Coze provides bots meant to make professional chores simpler. According to the Google Play store, Cici is the most downloaded app to date with over 10 million downloads.The apps appear to be a part of ByteDance's efforts to compete with its competitors in the generative AI sector, coupled with the company's launch of an AI tool to produce short-form videos and alleged attempts to construct an AI image generator comparable to Midjourney and Dall-E. In September of last year, Facebook released a celebrity-focused chatbot line, and in April, Snap incorporated an artificial intelligence chatbot into its platform. With the support of its $10 billion agreement with OpenAI, Microsoft is building AI assistants for many of its software tools, Google is introducing a new language model dubbed Gemini to compete with GPT-4, and Amazon is incorporating generative AI products into its Alexa smart speaker. All of the main tech deadline.

7 Crucial Steps For Developing An Internet Brand in 2024

In 2024, there won't be a single key to building an online brand. Instead, numerous things must be done in unison. Because there are so many tools accessible, developing a brand online is luckily simpler than it has ever been. It is still not straightforward, however. It's also vital to remember that creating a brand takes time. It demands being ethically upright over time.In 2024, you may take the following measures to create and extend your online brand:

1. Create a Robust, Integrated Brand Identity

This requires coming up with a unique brand name, logo, and visual style that represents the core of your company's character and ideals. A consistent visual and linguistic depiction of a brand across all channels is known as a cohesive brand identity. It encompasses the purpose, values, character, and market positioning of the brand. Consistency, clarity, relevance, distinctiveness, authenticity, adaptability, and coherence are the main components of a good brand identity.Apple is a superb example of a corporation in the present day with a consistent corporate brand. The brand's distinctive and high-end merchandise are crucial to its identity. Its symbol, a simple apple with a bite out of it, is immediately distinctive and has come to signify top-notch technology. Apple's visual identity is a monochromatic black, white, and silver color palette with a clean, minimalist design approach.

2. Produce Material

Building your online brand means creating and delivering valuable, relevant, and entertaining material consistently. Blog posts, videos, photos, graphics, and other sorts of media may all come under this category. In 2024, video content development will become increasingly crucial in online content creation. In my perspective, video will always be king, particularly on social media.

3. Engage in Social Media Activity

In 2023, social media will be vital for having an online presence and establishing a relationship with your target market. Instagram, TikTok, YouTube, Facebook, and LinkedIn are the key platforms utilized for creating an online brand.Let's explore each in turn:

- **Instagram**

Generally utilized as a tool for community building,

Instagram is used by consumers to determine who to buy from or work with. In my view, Instagram is among the finest sites to make actual offline connections. Direct messages (DMs) that are intriguing and short could assist you in accomplishing this.

• <u>**TikTok**</u>

A video-based platform that enables users to tag, search, and achieve organic reach.

• **YouTube:** After Google, it is the second-largest search engine globally. An excellent method to boost your organic reach on YouTube is to have video content there. People use YouTube often for search   reasons.

YouTube Shorts, a service that challenges Reels and TikToks for films that are 60 seconds or less, is its most popular feature. In 2023, YouTube Shorts may aid you enhance brand exposure because of their large organic reach.

Facebook: To stay in front of people who already know you, a personal Facebook account is still vital. You don't want them to forget your identity or your occupation.

Facebook has built a huge user base over its more than 10 years of operation. The friends of the majority of folks have known them for a longer duration than on other platforms.

• LinkedIn

is a professional network that allows connections between individuals in relevant industries. Because of its tremendous organic reach, posting information there boosts brand exposure. Building your brand on social channels may be accomplished by posting and communicating with followers often.

4. Create An Expert Website

A well-crafted website is a crucial component of any Internet business. Keep it brief and clear, and make it simple for visitors to access the information they were seeking on your website. Customers are accustomed to analyzing firms online and judging their legitimacy and credibility. A lousy website that is outdated, sluggish, verbose, difficult to use, and slow will make visitors feel the same way about your firm.

5. Present Yourself as an Authority in the Field

Through blog posts, presentations, and social media videos, communicate your knowledge and thoughts to your audience. In your company, this may help create your brand as a trusted information source. Share your knowledge regularly online, especially on different social media sites, if you have it in your profession. Include a little bit of your personality and interests as well. You may create a bond with your audience by doing this.

6. Involve Your Audience

Developing relationships is just as vital to developing an online brand as content sharing. Encourage your followers to offer their thoughts and experiences by connecting with them via messages and comments. Make advantage of social networking platforms to develop virtual ties with individuals, which you may subsequently enhance offline. Make your first impressions on folks by posting comments on their posts and sending them messages.

7. Work Together With Other Influencers And Brands

Collaborating with other companies or influencers helps widen the reach of your brand and enhance your reputation in regional and national industries. Social media sites have options that enable you to work together with another account and obtain exposure to their audience while they do the same for you. This is a win-win scenario for both of you. One example of such a feature is Instagram collaborations. To retain the integrity of your brand identity, search for influencers and other firms that match your beliefs.You will surely develop a successful internet brand in 2024 and beyond by sticking to these recommendations and preserving consistency.

Chapter 3

Eleven Artificial Intelligence Tools for Real Estate That Every Real Estate Agent Should Have

Would you say that artificial intelligence (AI) is a fad, a trend, or the word of the future, or do you think it is all of these things? According to what we know at the moment, artificial intelligence technologies in the real estate market are a game-changer in the industry.Increasingly, artificial intelligence (AI) is becoming an indispensable component of the real estate industry. The use of this technology has the potential to transform real estate professionals like yourself into heroes overnight.It has the potential to enhance the experiences of customers and speed up processes. With its support, you will be able to sell residences and create posts on social media in a way that was not possible previously. This is an adaptable item!Let's get started and have a look at eleven of the most important artificial intelligence technologies for real estate that will be required of all realtors in the year 2024.

1. AI-Driven 3D Virtual Home Tour Platforms

3D Home Tours on Zillow AI Tools for Real Estate

Real estate brokers utilize Zillow to seek homes. But were you aware that they featured a few more features? To gain ideas for interior design, try the 3D Home Tours Generator. This is an AI-powered real estate solution that will simplify your burden as an agent.With the use of AI, this 3D generator can create virtual tours for your customers. Any real estate business may use it to promote and sell houses.Investors in commercial real estate profit the most from it. This is because they typically desire rapid and economical virtual tours of vast estates.With this tool, half the job is completed. This is the URL to Zillow's 3D Generator.

2. Virtual House Flip Generators & Virtual Staging Solutions

Forget about employing pricey designers when it comes to understanding a property's potential. Alternatively, ignore them when launching your real estate firm.Virtual staging technologies driven by

AI, such as Virtual Staging, are valuable. Utilize AI real estate tactics to transform vacant land into fitted dwellings. To enhance house sales and attract more buyers, make use of such assets.You may even construct a home from the ground up with a virtual house flip. For individuals who restore and flip properties, this tool is a hidden gem. If you want to reinvent a house and let your creativity run wild, this new tool is a fantastic alternative.

3. Automated Content Marketing Automation with Xara Cloud, Xara Cloud-Powered Real Estate Marketing Materials

Producing outstanding real estate marketing material may be tough. Another problem is categorizing them and taking formats, channels, captions, etc. into consideration. Xara can handle all areas of content marketing management for your print publications and social media updates. **How**? Let Xara import your brand guidelines (logos, fonts, colors) by simply copying the URL of your website. They are also adjustable from within the dashboard. You will only set your name and personal brand once on the Personal Smartfields dashboard. After that, it will apply to all templates automatically!

Brand Administration for Xara Real Estate

Select from a range of customizable real estate templates.You're done when you apply your brand standards! Observe how the template converts into personalized information that is prepared for publication.Import the URL of your listing website with a few clicks to start advertising it. Xara instantly fills in any template with the contents of your ad, including images and information. Next, suggest that Xara AI write a new, compelling AI listing description. You have the right content produced for advertising your listing.With Xara's repurposing feature, you can effortlessly make an unlimited number of marketing materials. As building blocks, business-ready templates ensure you never have to start from zero. While the branding tool preserves the integrity of your brand's message, automated scaling assures that your content matches every medium.Utilize Open-AI-powered Xara's AI text generator to enrich your writing or even start fresh when generating your content. As an alternative, you may view the ready-to-use templates in Xara Cloud, which will be utilized by our AI tool. To begin integrating AI into your real estate strategy, check out Xara! utilize AI to populate social media posts or prints that you make from templates and utilize them instantly.

4. Chatbots Powered by AI Tidy Real Estate AI Tools

Chatbots that employ conversational AI, like Tidio, exhibit the capacity of artificial intelligence. Customer service in the real estate market is being changed by this device.An AI bot is capable of the following:

- ★ **Interact with prospective customers**
- ★ **Respond to requests from clients**
- ★ **Arrange for property visits.**
- ★ **Boost conversions by giving highly personalized interactions and ideas.**
- ★ **AI chatbots may recollect prior discussions.**

As a consequence, they may directly follow up with prospects by asking questions such as, "Is this a better time? You indicated earlier that you had an event organized, I think. How did things work out? Chatbots are really helpful when it comes to digital real estate

5. AI Tools for Predictive Analytics in House Canary Real Estate Pricing

Any real estate firm may profit from implementing AI solutions like Redfin and HouseCanary. When it comes to applying valuation algorithms to price homes, they give a competitive edge.They study a lot of data, including prior sales, market trends, and property qualities. Realtors may then utilize the information to determine the optimal listing price. Put a stop to spending hours and money on market reports!The experience of acquiring a house has also been drastically revolutionized by the usage of AI in real estate. AI algorithms are utilized by organizations like Zillow to enhance their estimate.That is one approach to gaining more accurate property prices.Overall, artificial intelligence (AI) technology exceeds human brains. That is, at least, the case when calculating, analyzing, and concurrently interpreting a large quantity of data. Why not employ AI-driven real estate technologies to learn about property values?

6. Customer relationship management (CRM) boosted by AI

AI Tools for Real Estate at Lion Desk

All real estate organizations may benefit from AI to increase their CRM (customer relationship management). That's what various AI real estate solutions do. Among them are Property Base, WiseAgent, and LionDesk.They evaluate interactions, preferences, and behaviors using machine-learning approaches. What they can achieve is as follows:

Customized Advice Regarding Properties

AI is capable of producing suggestions for properties depending on the tastes of certain clients. It does this by examining past data and consumer behavior. Imagine a real estate matching app powered by AI. AI is capable of providing recommendations that outperform the user's search parameters.

Sentiment analysis of customers in real-time

Real-time AI analysis of client input, including sentiment analysis and open-ended comments, is conceivable. Real estate businesses are therefore able to predict client behavior and satisfy their expectations.

Customer Communication

Chatbots with AI skills may aid customers even in the absence of live chat professionals. They may react to questions from clients, schedule showings, and offer up-to-date property data. Best Time to Reach Out. Compass and other CRM software employ artificial intelligence (AI) to assist decide when to contact customers. Through client activities and website interactions, the system may gather user information. After that, it may prod you with a "likely to sell" indicator for every customer.

AI is capable of real things. For lasting loyalty, employ it to boost client connections and the customer experience.

7. Predictive Maintenance Assisted by AI

Forge Honeywell Artificial Intelligence for Property Upkeep

Predictive maintenance systems with artificial intelligence, like Honeywell Forge, are a tremendous benefit for real estate development organizations. The gadget employs data analysis from a range of sensors to predict maintenance issues before they arise.As a consequence, there are fewer unanticipated repairs and properties remain in good form.

8. Market Analysis Driven by AI

Property Intelligence in Reonomy AI

Artificial intelligence is employed by platforms such as Reonomy to propose investment possibilities to real estate agents. These technologies give you all the knowledge you need to plan your next move by analyzing large amounts of data.Those in the real estate sector that do not employ artificial intelligence will be at a competitive disadvantage. The last thing you want as an agent or brokerage is that. Therefore, you need to start entrusting AI to spot trends and propose the finest brokers to your team.Utilize your personnel resources more efficiently. They are capable of conducting original real estate marketing and qualified lead creation. Let AI extract important insights from manual activities like data analysis and online search research.

9. AI-Powered Lead Creation Tools for Zillow Premier Agent Real Estate

Platforms for producing leads utilizing AI, such as BoldLeads and Zillow Premier Agent, are fantastic. To discover and target new consumers, they deploy AI algorithms. Finding new clients is made much easier by looking at demographics and internet behavior.Exclusive listing placements and customized agent websites are given by **Zillow Premier Agent.** These bring in customer leads according to various places. Automation is utilized by **BoldLeads CRM** to speed lead generation activities.Artificial intelligence changes lead generation and frees you up to focus on high-potential consumers.Real estate farming is another approach that AI may be utilized to provide leads. How? Well, homeowners may identify the finest real estate agents with the aid of AI-driven tools like **Houzen**. They achieve this by filtering realtors. Based on accreditations, local expertise, and success rates, this takes happen.Being a thought leader in your sector will therefore be advantageous when clients are hunting for the greatest agent accessible.

10. Artificial Intelligence-Based Personal Assistant Luke Real Estate AI Tools

Real estate agents have a significant competitive advantage because of AI-powered personal assistants. Similar to having a next-door assistant, however, AI is more efficient at it. programs such as Gabbi, Deal Machine's Alma, and Luke. Among the greatest virtual assistants for real estate is AI. A smart AI assistant is capable of:

- ❖ **Simplify your labor.**
- ❖ **Improve the way you interact with consumers.**

❖ Offer intelligent criticism.

❖ Cross items off your list of tasks to achieve.

❖ Set reminders and plan meetings.

❖ To maximize conversions, take charge of cold emailing and generate targeted content.

And a whole lot more!Natural language processing is utilized by AI assistants to interpret prospect questions and offer automated responses. They may organize excursions, obtain information from possible consumers, and even check into market trends.They also run around the clock. This makes it feasible to instantly engage clients even when human staff are not on duty.

11. Intelligent Solution for Workflow and Asset Management

Asset Management & Workflow Solution from IBM

IBM An AI system named TRIRIGA assists in the administration of workplaces and buildings. This platform is innovative for the commercial real estate market. TRIRIGA is a solution for intelligent asset management. It is a component of an IWMS, or integrated workplace management system.It satisfies the needs of current facilities management by combining AI and data. It may expedite operations linked to real estate and facilities management and manage workplaces and buildings.

Some of IBM TRIRIGA's primary benefits are:

Instantaneous sensations enable flexible spatial organization. This allows renters to book rooms and make service requests.

simplifying the administration of leases and saving expenditures

Enhancing Performance

Preventative maintenance

Improving energy efficiency to minimize carbon emissions

The flexible management of building lifecycles is made feasible by TRIRIGA's solution. It is an excellent resource for any commercial real estate organization as it also assists in future requirement preparedness.

AI in Real Estate: What Does It Mean?

The real estate business is transforming owing to artificial intelligence. It offers realtors with a variety of tools to optimize operations and increase customer relations. AI is the future of the real estate market, not merely a fashionable word or slogan. Here are some ways AI is affecting real estate in the future:

Increased Productivity. AI-powered instruments make labor simpler. They may minimize manual work, enhance lead generation, improve customer service, and provide virtual home tours, among other things.

Individualization. You may deliver tailored marketing content and property ideas due to AI.

Making Well-Informed Decisions. Tools for market analysis and predictive analytics give useful information. They enable you to make data-driven decisions regarding investment possibilities and pricing.

Improved Customer Experience. Chatbots and personal assistants powered by AI offer round-the-clock help, boosting contact with consumers.

An advantage over the competition. Using AI gives agents a competitive edge. It may facilitate lead creation and enhance the proportion of finished agreements.

Future-Readiness. Real estate agents may better prepare for the future of the industry by adopting AI.

AI will keep growing vital in marketing, customer service, and property management.

Real Estate Brokers

Embracing Change Is Difficult Yet Well Worth It

Without a doubt, artificial intelligence is the way of the future for the real estate business. These 11 AI technologies are vital, ranging from virtual staging to property search websites.Adopting AI technology increases client experiences while simplifying operations. It promotes data analysis, enhanced decision-making, and the creation of effective business models. They are pretty good in this aspect as well.

How Can I Make Effective Use of Online Property Listings?

The search for the perfect dwelling has grown in unison with the advent of new technologies in today's fast-paced world. The days of driving around neighborhoods searching for **"For Sale"** signs and going over multiple newspaper listings in quest of a property to buy are long gone. You may locate the house that best matches your criteria with simplicity by searching online property listings. We'll walk you through the processes necessary to properly take advantage of the chances presented by online real estate listings in this book section. Now, let's begin this exciting trip, The Revolution in Real Estate Listings Online.In recent years, the real estate industry has witnessed a tremendous shift owing to the advent of Internet property listings. Now that time and physical location are no longer barriers, prospective homeowners may browse a broad choice of properties at their leisure. Real estate websites have quickly taken the place of other websites when someone is searching to acquire a new home to reside in. It's simpler than ever to identify the home of your dreams owing to the big inventory and extensive information.

A Manual for Efficient Internet Real Estate Lookups

It is customary to overlook these developments in the fast-changing real estate sector. By personalizing their notifications, users of Property Online may make sure they are among the first to know when a property that fulfills their specifications is made available.Users of Property Online may take advantage of special virtual property tours. It's a good idea to browse the area where you already dwell and check the floor plans before you organize in-person visits. Additionally, enjoy a thorough view from balconies.While internet real estate listings could give some valuable information, interacting with a registered real estate specialist can provide much more. You may contact skilled real estate agents via Property Online, and they may guide you through the complete house-buying process.

1. Imagining the Interior of Your Dream House

Clearly describe your ideal house before searching through internet real estate listings. What material objects are "must-haves" and "nice-to-haves" for you? Think about crucial criteria like the location of the property, the number of bedrooms, and the price range. Similarly, Property Online features sophisticated search criteria that speed the process of finding a better match while also saving you time.

2 Opting for the Right Operating System

Not every website offering properties for sale is made equal. Likewise, your ability to pick the ideal platform will decide how successful you are. Property Online sets itself apart from its rivals with its user-friendly appearance, huge property database, and exceptional reputation. Their listings are thorough, featuring both high-quality photographs and insightful information. It enables you to explore each home in its full.

3 Setting Up Alerts

The real estate market is characterized by rapid activity. Do not allow your tardiness in browsing the listings to cost you the house of your aspirations. On Property Online, you may set alerts for specified parameters. It assures you'll be among the first to hear when a new listing becomes available. And when something that meets your preferences becomes available.

Virtual Tours

By giving a unique feature like virtual tours, Property Online sets itself apart from its competition. Explore different communities without ever leaving the comforts of your own home. You are allowed to roam around the residence and enjoy the view from the balcony before opting to plan a real-life visit. and get a sense of how the rooms are structured.

5. Look for Expert Help

Avoid emphasizing the benefits of dealing with a registered real estate agent, even when going through internet property listings could give substantial information. You may connect with qualified real estate agents with a wealth of business knowledge by utilizing Property Online. They will support you through the house-buying process.

<u>Final Thoughts</u>

You may locate the perfect house of your dreams by looking through the various internet property listings that are at your disposal. Property Online makes the process simpler and the experience more fun with its huge property database and user-friendly website. Define your ideal house, hunt for a suitable platform, set up notifications, browse virtual tours, and consider about hiring expert aid. If you follow these directions, you will soon be well on your way to achieving your dream house.

Data Analytics's Significance in Digital Marketing

Since the middle of the 19th century, marketers have been reviewing their plans and methods; yet, the data analytics of today is significantly different from those early efforts at profit-maximizing marketing. Driven by digital technology, data analytics models estimate the value of each customer connection and interaction point across numerous channels and devices. With the use of advanced analytic tools, over 80% of marketing professionals base their judgments on data. They examine digital marketing activities at every level of the customer experience.Those who can successfully utilize these sophisticated tools to gather insightful marketing data will lead the way in digital strategy going ahead. This section digs deeper into the issue of data analytics in digital marketing, outlining what it is, where the data comes from, and how it may be utilized to enhance the success of digital marketing initiatives.

What Is Data Analytics in Digital Marketing?

The process of gathering and interpreting data from many digital sources to acquire practical insights about a business's digital marketing approaches is known as data analytics in the marketing industry. By offering a tailored experience, digital marketing analytics solutions may minimize churn rate—the proportion of consumers who stop doing business with a company—and enhance the value of present customers.2,3 According to a 2020 corporate analytics report, barely 30% of firms have a clear data strategy, despite 94% of organizations perceiving data and analytics as crucial to their digital transformation and success.By removing the uncertainty of marketing strategy and increasing the return on investment from a company's marketing budget, data analytics helps organizations function more effectively.

Which Three Marketing Analytics Models Are There?

Three main types of analytical models are used by professional marketers to plan, analyze, and enhance their marketing operations.

Descriptive: Previous campaign data is acquired, and this information is utilized to give insight and help the development of campaign methods for the following campaigns.

Prescriptive: These models gather data from all available touchpoints, measuring the effect of each corporate activity and customer encounter to enable the firm to design highly focused campaigns that affect consumer behavior.

Predictive: These data analytics algorithms strive to forecast consumers' behavior using information from prior marketing initiatives.When integrated, these analytical models give a full picture of the success of marketing campaigns and teach each organization how to work toward its objectives more effectively.

Where Is the Source of the Data?

Many various sources offer raw data for digital analytics, which may be difficult for a corporation without the internal know-how to manage it. Sources of information on customer interactions include:

Data from websites (tracking)Product information (features most/least desired, conversion events, and friction spots)Information from digital marketing (keyword research, social media interactions)Internal customer information (transactions, complaints, and accounts). This sort of information may now be acquired in real-time without communicating with clients directly.

The Application of Marketing Analytics

Data analytics is a technology used by marketers to assess enormous volumes of customer data and deliver insights that drive their brand, product strategy, and advertising initiatives.Businesses may acquire a better grasp of their sector and clients by adopting modern data analytics approaches. This may result in more effective digital marketing strategies, individualized customer experiences, greater customer satisfaction, increased productivity, and higher profitability.

Create Detailed Profiles of Your Customers

It is possible to observe the full user experience in one area by merging data from multiple sources. You may observe, for instance, how people reach your website via adverts, social media, etc. All of their activity, including product purchases and inquiries, are also available to you. The full client lifecycle—from an unmet need and understanding of your products or services to contact with your firm, purchase, and engagement—can be revealed to you using data analytics. These same customers might even go on to suggest the product or service to others by informing them about their excellent experiences.

Match Product Outperformance to the Expectations of Customers

Your company's marketing personnel may better align product features and marketing efforts with customer expectations by leveraging actionable data to ensure improved results. This may lower the rate of attrition.

Recognize consumer behavior

Understanding and predicting consumer behavior patterns may help you adjust your marketing and advertising efforts to their desires, which is a critical ability for customer acquisition. Mail marketing solutions, for instance, enable you to track subscribers and see their reactions, such as likes and shares on social media. Increased sales are the outcome of increasing customer participation.

Create Novel Product Features, Innovative Approaches, and Fresh Revenue Sources.

A business may experiment with client acquisition more safely if it has access to up-to-date consumer preference data. Based on what the data says about the client's desires, it may build a new product, enhance an existing one, or establish a new marketing campaign. It might also open the door to additional kinds of income.

Establish Targeted Customization

According to a Google marketing survey, 90% of experienced marketers agreed that more income may be created by customized marketing. You may produce highly targeted content by employing the extensive client information offered by marketing analytics. Based on user profiles, prior purchases, and browsing behaviors, analytics software may anticipate and detect client preferences, enhancing the entire customer experience.

Track the efficacy of campaigns

You can evaluate the efficacy of your marketing efforts in real time with suitable analytics tools, which makes your organization more nimble when it comes to campaign optimization and plan refining. Because it helps you to get the most out of your advertising expenditure, this is especially vital for sponsored marketing efforts. Marketing campaigns may thus be quickly connected to major indications, such as the number of visitors to your company's website, and you can examine the effect of various marketing channels (web, mobile, social media, etc.) on customer behavior. This may then assist in boosting efficiency and direct future initiatives.In the marketing business, ROI (return on investment) is vital. By correlating a business's marketing activities to ROI, marketing analytics helps to justify its marketing expense.

Anticipated Need

You may spot patterns and trends and predict demand for products and services by studying up-to-date data and examining records. The capacity to estimate future occurrences is offered by predictive analytics, which may be highly valuable for enterprises, especially those working on a tight budget. With digital marketing, data analytics provides your organization with a competitive advantage. You may utilize it to obtain a greater grasp of not simply your organization and clients, but also the settings in which they work. The information may be utilized to establish marketing strategies, pull in new customers, maintain existing ones, identify unsuccessful marketing campaigns, and focus on your best-performing things. Additionally, you may utilize web analytics tools to discover more about your rivals. Keeping your firm informed about the industry helps you prepare for future difficulties and alter your marketing to better match customer sentiment.

What Kind of Skills Are Necessary for Marketing Analytics?

There's a lot to learn about data analytics in digital marketing. You'll surely need statistical analysis and data visualization skills, as well as creative capabilities like copywriting, content development, and storytelling, to be effective in digital marketing analytics yourself and properly explain your findings. Additionally, you should know how to utilize data analytics tools like **Semrush** for campaign analytics and Google Analytics for website analytics. Metrics including website traffic, customer retention rates, cost per click, conversion rates, sales revenue, social media engagement, and more are collected by these technologies. Six These professional talents are important to comprehend how to evaluate all this data, and having this insight may dramatically boost a company's bottom line.

Invest in your empowerment with an online MSBA to progress.

Acquire the talents that are in demand today to better your career. The William & Mary Online Master of Science in Business Analytics (MSBA) program is focused on business acumen, quantitative modeling, computer technology (especially, major data analytics languages and Python), and compelling communication. It is aimed at working professionals. You will cover business analytics, cloud computing, big data analysis, optimization, prescriptive analytics, machine learning, and predictive analysis in great depth.

The Nine Richest Real Estate Specialties and Their Rationale

A realtor analyzes the most successful real estate markets and the reasons for their success while reclining on the couch.Working smarter, not harder, is the key to success as a real estate salesman. And focusing on a particular real estate niche is among your greatest selections.Adhering to a single real estate specialization may initially appear restricting, but there are several benefits to doing so. You may focus your attention, generate incredibly targeted and convincing content, position yourself as the go-to expert, and build your real estate agency by specializing in a given subject.

What is a niche in real estate?

Real estate agents need to pick a real estate specialization. The best-paying real estate markets and the reasons behind them. A real estate specialty is the particular industry you select to concentrate on becoming an expert in. One may carve out an unlimited number of niches, such as situational or location-based (we'll go into more detail about the most profitable real estate niches a little later). It's vital to focus on a real estate niche that compliments your skill set and is something you wish to commit your time to.

Why real estate agents need to pick a real estate specialization

Discovering your real estate specialization provides several rewards. For instance, focussing on a single topic helps you to grow and become an expert in that sector, better understand your target market, and build eye-catching advertising campaigns.Having real estate expertise also helps you stand out and be distinct from other brokers. 76% of buyers in 2023 purchased their homes via a real estate agent or broker, and 39% of purchasers indicated that having an agent help them in locating the appropriate property was what they most wanted. You may separate yourself from other generalist agents who may not have the same degree of expertise in the real estate sector by becoming an expert in it.The best-paying real estate markets and the reasons behind them

The four real estate niches with the highest income potential are location (e.g., a specific city or region), demographics (e.g., veterans and military personnel), property type (e.g., distressed properties, luxury homes, or real estate-owned inventory), and situation (e.g., horse owners or divorcing couples).

Real estate specialty based on location

Not surprisingly, the most popular real estate specialism is location. This could be determined by a zip code, town, county, or neighborhood. Real estate agents that specialize in various locations may be a valuable source of knowledge about their local markets. For instance, a real estate agent with a specialty in downtown houses would have a solid awareness of the expectations of both buyers and sellers in this market. Agents may focus on their lead generation and marketing efforts to target the correct audience by having a confined geographical concentration.

Real estate niches based on demography

Real estate agents could also profit from specializing in demographic real estate markets. One approach would be to focus on catering to a specific group, such as first-time homeowners, millennials, real estate investors, or veterans of the military services.

You may become an expert at addressing the needs, wants, and issues of that target demographic by delivering specialized services to a restricted market group. Another wonderful technique to generate referrals and build your real estate agency is to carve out a demographic-based real estate expertise.

Real estate specializations focusing on properties

Creating your real estate expertise around a specific sort of property is another sensible option to consider. **You might desire to concentrate on luxury houses, rental properties, hotels, REO and foreclosures, and other specialized property types.**

Consider a real estate agent who specializes in rentals, for instance. According to statistics from the National Multifamily Housing Council, 44 million households in the US are renters. A realtor may gain an in-depth insight into the local rental market, including leasing interest and pricing, by concentrating on rentals. They might become renowned as the landlords' favorite agency when it comes to locating suitable renters and negotiating leases. Furthermore, there are booming rental markets for single-family homes and even luxury residences in some regions, so a rental niche isn't solely confined to towns with an abundance of flats.

If you wish to study this idea further, you can consider completing a Rental Market Analysis (RMA). This could aid you in assessing whether renting out properties might be a successful real estate expertise for your firm.

Situational markets for real estate

A situational real estate expertise, such as divorce and separation, probate and estates, or equestrian properties, is another option for brokers to explore.

An agent well-versed in estate proceedings, for example, may help clients through the legal and financial complications of these transactions with ease. In a similar vein, an agent with equestrian knowledge may help a buyer ask the necessary questions and find the appropriate sorts of houses to visit by relying on their understanding of land and stables.

Other specialties in real estate

Real estate brokers have access to a broad variety of real estate specializations, even if the aforementioned are the most well-liked and profitable ones at the present. Realtors may learn a lot about new or growing niches by utilizing their creativity and keeping an eye on regional and national real estate trends. Other real estate specialty that may be discovered include:

<u>Eco-friendly houses</u>

Eco-friendly houses that highlight sustainability and environmental concerns are the major focus of this real estate specialization.

Fresh Building

This specialist area provides site selection, design, and construction services to buyers and real estate investors wishing to acquire or build a new house.

Historical establishments

Whether evaluating historic Victorian houses, stately manors, or commercial buildings, this expertise covers the complexities that buyers, sellers, and real estate investors must negotiate.

Agricultural characteristics

This branch of expertise focuses on agriculturally-oriented investment assets, such as farmsteads, vineyards, and orchards.Real estate agents may identify a specialization that matches with their interests, talents, and resources by studying these and other niches. Whichever industry you decide on, it's vital to know your target real estate market properly and be able to give them the services they desire. Your consumers should have confidence in you as a competent and trustworthy partner, regardless of whether you specialize in new construction for real estate investors or historical residences for divorcées.

Using your real estate specialty

Alright, so you've selected the real estate market niche that appeals to you. How can you put it into practice now? Since it will help you stand out from the competition and attract your target customer, your specialization should serve as the cornerstone of all your marketing endeavors.It's vital to design a marketing message that appeals to your target demographic. It's vital to understand their wants and objectives to successfully and convincingly communicate with them. A very effective place to start is by applying the PFDD framework to define your ideal customer profile (ICP). Take into mind the following marketing tactics to adequately promote your real estate niche:

Ads in paid media

One of the most effective methods to connect potential clients in your sector is to execute highly targeted advertising via social media and paid search. You should also consider leveraging digital and print media in your neighborhood.

Make a website for real estate.

Make sure your website is professional, user-friendly, and well-designed as it's frequently the first impression that potential buyers will receive of you. Make sure to display your area of expertise and supply potential consumers with relevant and valuable information.Writing articles, filming videos, and blogging are all intelligent marketing strategies that show off your skills and pull in new consumers.Making insightful instructional resources that apply to your real estate specialization will help you become identified as a dependable authority.

Social networks

Social media networks with major marketing potential include Facebook, Instagram, and

LinkedIn. Utilize them to develop contacts with possible clients, convey your expertise and experience, and publicize your listings.

Email promotion

Creating an email list of subscribers who are interested in your real estate specialism will help you to connect with potential consumers more effectively. Sending out frequent email newsletters with informative information and updates on your listings could help you stay at the top of your audience's thoughts.

These are just a few of the various marketing tactics you may use to promote your real estate expertise, connect and engage with your target audience, and build your real estate firm.

In summary

Real estate agents may prosper by finding and utilizing a real estate specialist. You may become an expert in that area, give greater client service, and build your real estate firm by specializing in a specific real estate market or location.Regardless of the real estate specialization you choose to focus on before you begin, be sure you've done your study. Even though it might take some time to get underway, making intelligent selections today will pay dividends in the long term.

Chapter 4

HOW TO GET THE BEST DEAL FROM A DISTANCE DURING REMOTE REAL ESTATE NEGOTIATIONS

Overseeing remote real estate transactions presents a distinct set of challenges and opportunities. The way we buy and sell real estate has evolved over the years, making it possible to search for the ideal home or investment regardless of geographical distance. Now, let's examine the methods and variables that will help you get the best deal when you're at a distance!

Comprehending the remote real Estate negotiations

When we look closely at the intricacy of remote real estate conversations, we can see how technology has changed the way we think about buying a house. Thanks to the advent of virtual property tours and internet listings, purchasers may now save time and effort by seeing homes from the comfort of their screens. This suggests that identifying important criteria for your ideal home ahead of time, including location's importance, is much easier. Realizing the potential drawbacks and restrictions, such as relying only on digital representations, is crucial. This tactic makes things easier, but it requires adaptability.

Thus, it's still crucial to strike a balance between using technology and keeping a thorough understanding of a property's actual situation. It's critical to embrace the benefits and steer clear of the hazards of this shifting landscape to get the best deal.

Locating the top real estate representative

A knowledgeable and reliable agent might provide important market information. In addition, they might teach you about the difficulties involved in buying a home or even negotiate well on your behalf. Furthermore, it is possible to get information about hiring interstate movers and moving from Michigan to Florida by having a reliable realtor on the scene, allowing you to delegate the process to a professional team! They may be able to recommend reliable interstate moving companies and provide you with assistance with your move. Therefore, an experienced agent is also a wonderful resource for handling the more complex aspects of your move. As a result, take into account expertise, familiarity with the area, and commitment to your needs while searching for the ideal real estate agent.

Virtual inspections and tours of properties

A crucial element of remote real estate transactions is virtual property tours and inspections, which make it easier to choose the ideal home for you. They save time and effort by allowing buyers to take comprehensive virtual tours of homes from the comfort of their screens. Without going inside, you can examine every inch of them, including the spacious yard and the elegant living room. Additionally, you may ask detailed questions about the property to get insight into its condition during virtual inspections. It's a crucial tool for narrowing down your options and expressing interest in properties that fit your needs.

Haggling about the cost

One of the most important steps in the purchase of real estate is price negotiation. It takes more than just asking for less money; it takes finding the right middle ground that benefits the seller as well as the buyer. Using the previously stated virtual tours to be ready for negotiations about repairs and other similar concerns and their impact on the final price is also a crucial part of the process. Having a comprehensive knowledge of a property allows you to enter into talks knowing exactly what needs to be fixed or changed. This might lower the total price and provide you with a discount. As an alternative, you might even suggest that the seller agree to take care of some of the problems and repairs in advance.

Vigilance and record-keeping

A thorough due diligence process includes researching the property's background, making sure it meets your needs, and finding out its legal standing. To identify any issues, this process includes reviewing survey results, property records, and inspection reports. Zoning regulations, easements, and other encumbrances that can restrict the use of the land must be carefully considered. Regarding documentation, buying or selling real estate requires a significant amount of it. Carefully reading and accurately executing contracts, deeds, mortgage agreements, and disclosure statements are essential. Document errors or omissions might cause financial and legal problems once you're probably shut down. Naturally, working with an experienced real estate lawyer or agent may be quite helpful in navigating this sensitive part of the transaction.

Mortgage and financing factors

Getting financing for the purchase of a house is a challenging process that calls for scrutiny. It is essential to comprehend mortgage rates, terms, and conditions to make informed investing decisions. Additionally,, this might have a significant impact on the resources available to you when it comes time to be ready for your move. Your overall budget, long-term financial stability, and monthly payments may all be directly impacted by the mortgage you choose. As a result, it's essential to compare many loan options and shop around for the best mortgage rates. You may choose a mortgage that meets your financial goals with confidence in this way.

Completing the deal

Finalizing the transaction signifies the conclusion of a successful real estate negotiation and the final steps toward obtaining property ownership. This process involves reviewing the necessary documentation and resolving any outstanding contingencies. There are many formalities involved in the process, including contract signatures, money transfers, and property condition inspections. As part of due diligence, it is essential to confirm that all documentation is accurate and complies with local laws. You may also arrange for remote closings, which allow the sale to close more quickly even if the parties are located in different locations. You get the keys to the house and ownership when you meet all the requirements and pay the closing costs.

Safeguard a property from a distance with assurance.

Our attitude to property negotiations has changed as a result of how easy remote real estate conversations are to use. You can overcome the challenges and seize the opportunity if you embrace technology and practice careful planning and effective communication! Therefore, regardless of the physical distance, the strategies discussed in this article may help you get the best price, whether you're investing or buying the property of your dreams. New avenues have been created by remote real estate deals, and you may bravely navigate them if you use the right approach!

Chapter 5

Escrow Account Administration

Optimal Techniques for Monetary Achievement

The Value of Managing an Escrow Account

Effective administration of escrow accounts is essential for achieving financial success as it protects from potential threats, instills trust, and guarantees the smooth execution of financial transactions. This section delves into the complex world of escrow account management, examining its applicability from a variety of perspectives. Whether you are a buyer, seller, or business owner, mastering the management of escrow accounts might revolutionize your financial journey.

1. Risk mitigation: When two parties are involved in a financial transaction, escrow accounts function as a safety net. Let's say you are buying a house.

The buyer is protected from any contract violations and the seller is guaranteed access to the funds by placing the purchase payment in an escrow account. The customer may get their money back if the seller fails to fulfill their obligations.

2. building trust: Every financial transaction is based on the establishment of trust. Money held in escrow communicates to all parties concerned the seriousness and dependability of the deal. With the assurance that their money is safe, this guarantee may persuade hesitant buyers to complete the transaction or encourage vendors to fulfill their end of the bargain.

3. Legal Compliance: In certain transactions, especially those involving real estate, escrow accounts are usually required by law. Maintaining adherence to these guidelines can save you legal troubles and create an environment that is honest and moral for your financial dealings.

4. Transactions are executed quickly and seamlessly, which is one of the main advantages of using escrow accounts. Before releasing the funds, the escrow agent confirms that all contract conditions have been met. As a result, neither the seller nor the buyer must pursue the other for their share of the transaction.

5. Success in Online Marketplaces: The need for escrow accounts is even more critical in the age of online marketplaces. For example, in a high-value eBay transaction, the buyer does not pay the seller directly. Rather, the payments are deposited into an escrow account, and they are only released to the vendor if the customer receives the products as agreed. By doing this, fraud is eliminated and confidence in online transactions is increased.

6. Escrow Agents: Professionals or companies referred to as escrow agents often oversee escrow accounts. These middlemen are essential to guaranteeing that the contract's terms and conditions are met. They are essential in complex transactions because they provide impartiality and expertise to the process.

7. long-term advantages: Escrow account management encompasses more than just one-time deals. It could be essential to creating long-lasting business relationships. By using escrow accounts consistently, you show that you are committed to safe and truthful transactions, which might result in referrals and repeat business.

8. Cost distribution: Escrow accounts may be used in particular situations, like real estate, to distribute costs like property taxes and insurance premiums. This eliminates potential issues by enabling each party to contribute fairly.

Knowing why escrow account management is important goes beyond simple money transactions. It has to do with maintaining legal compliance, fostering seamless transactions, managing risk, and building trust. You may ensure financial success and create enduring business relationships by using best practices and utilizing escrow agents' knowledge.

Developing Explicit Policies and Processes for Escrow Account Administration

Establishing precise guidelines and procedures for handling escrow accounts is essential to ensuring financial success. An escrow account is a kind of financial arrangement in which two parties involved in a transaction entrust their funds to a third party. The interests of the seller and the buyer are protected by this account, which serves as a protection. But if there aren't any established guidelines or procedures, keeping these accounts up to date might become challenging and even dangerous.Precise guidelines and procedures for maintaining an escrow account provide buyers with peace of mind. They promise that their funds are kept secure and are delivered only once all predetermined requirements have been met. Since both parties are aware that the money is being handled honestly and properly, this fosters trust between the buyer and the seller. Furthermore, unambiguous guidelines and procedures aid in avoiding any miscommunications or conflicts that can arise throughout the transaction process.Establishing clear guidelines and procedures for escrow account upkeep is beneficial from the seller's perspective as well. It guarantees that the buyer's funds are readily available and will be released right away after meeting the predetermined requirements. This facilitates a seamless conclusion and helps to streamline the transaction process. Furthermore, strict guidelines and procedures support the seller's professional reputation by demonstrating a commitment to moral and responsible financial practices.Take into consideration the following best practices when creating explicit guidelines and procedures for managing escrow accounts:

1. Record the process: Write down all the steps involved in keeping escrow accounts in a comprehensive document. Provide information on the methods used to receive, verify, and retain funds as well as the requirements for releasing them. All parties involved should have easy access to this document, which should be updated often to reflect modifications made to the procedure.

2. Duties and Responsibilities: Clearly state what each individual involved in managing the escrow account is expected to do. This includes the escrow agency, the buyer, the seller, and any other pertinent parties. Assign defined responsibilities to every stakeholder to ensure accountability and minimize misinterpretation.

3. Create Verification procedures: Put in place thorough verification procedures to ensure that the funds received are legitimate and meet the predetermined criteria. This might include doing due diligence on each party involved in the transaction, verifying the accuracy of the documentation, and investigating the source of the funds.

4. Maintain Accurate Records: Make sure you have thorough documentation of all discussions and transactions about the escrow account. Invoices, contracts, receipts, and any other relevant paperwork fall under this category. Maintaining accurate records is essential for audits, resolving disputes, and guaranteeing transparency at every stage of the process.

5. Rules should be reviewed and updated regularly since escrow account management procedures change with time. As a result, your procedures and rules should also be. To maintain the compliance and effectiveness of your escrow account management, be informed on regulatory changes and industry best practices.Imagine, for instance, a real estate transaction in which the buyer puts money into an escrow account that won't be released until the seller does the necessary repairs. The specific requirements for disbursing the funds, together with the deadline for finishing the repairs and the supporting documentation to prove their accomplishment, would be clearly defined by standards and procedures. By doing this, you can make sure that everyone is aware of their responsibilities and avoid misunderstandings or delays in the transaction process.Achieving financial success requires establishing certain policies and procedures for managing escrow accounts. These guidelines provide a framework for transparent and accountable financial management, building trust between

Efficient Client and Stakeholder Communication in Escrow Account Management

Good customer and stakeholder communication is essential in the field of escrow account management. Establishing unambiguous channels of communication is essential for financial experts to ensure financial success, foster confidence, and ensure transparency. The secret to creating wonderful connections and guaranteeing smooth transactions is effective communication, whether you are working with clients, banks, lawyers, or other stakeholders.To guarantee that the client's needs and expectations are met throughout the escrow procedure, good communication is essential. Building trust and confidence with your consumers may be achieved by providing regular updates and promptly addressing any concerns or questions. Clear communication on the funds' status, the progress of the transaction, and any potential roadblocks will allay client concerns and foster a positive working relationship.However, effective communication with all parties involved in the escrow process—banks, lawyers, and other parties—is just as important. By keeping everyone involved and aware, you can reduce miscommunication, holdups, and potential conflicts. Maintaining open lines of communication may help ensure that everyone is working toward the same goal and is in agreement.Examine the following suggested strategies to improve your communication abilities while managing escrow accounts:

1. Engage in active listening to fully understand the needs, concerns, and expectations of your stakeholders and consumers. You could establish rapport and forge stronger ties by demonstrating empathy and comprehension. For instance, if a client raises concerns about the safety of their money, pay attention to what they have to say and reassure them

by outlining the strong security measures that are in place.

2. Clear and succinct Communication: When speaking with stakeholders and consumers, use language that is both clear and succinct. Steer clear of technical terms or jargon that might alienate or confuse them. Make sure that everyone involved understands the material by presenting it understandably. For example, when explaining the escrow process to a client, explain each step using simple terms and examples.

3. timely updates: Let your stakeholders and clients know how the escrow process is progressing regularly. Depending on their preferences, this may be accomplished via meetings, phone calls, or emails. You demonstrate professionalism and transparency by providing frequent updates. For instance, notify all parties involved as soon as there are any delays or issues that might influence the timeline to manage expectations.

4. Encourage open, two-way communication with your stakeholders and consumers. Establish an environment where individuals are at ease sharing their thoughts, worries, and critiques. When it is possible, actively seek their counsel and include them in the decision-making process. This cooperative strategy could foster trust and enhance the whole encounter. For example, after going over the details of an escrow agreement with a client, get their opinion and address any queries or worries they may have.

5. Use of Technology: make better use of technology to increase productivity and enhance communication processes. Use secure online ways to share documents, updates, and other relevant data. Time is saved, and important data security and confidentiality are guaranteed. Ease and transparency may be achieved, for instance, by offering clients access to real-time information about their escrow accounts via a client portal.An essential component of managing escrow accounts is effective communication. You may establish strong relationships with stakeholders and consumers by actively listening, speaking in plain and understandable terms, providing frequent updates, encouraging two-way contact, and using technology. In addition to making the overall experience better, following these suggested practices will support the growth and profitability of your escrow account management business.

Putting Strict Security Measures in Place to Protect Escrow Accounts

Putting in Place a Robust Security System with Robust Security Measures. In today's financial sector, escrow account protection requires the establishment of complete security measures. Escrow accounts are an essential component of many financial transactions, including real estate sales, mergers and acquisitions, and online purchases. They hold funds for a specific purpose until certain conditions are met. Organizations and individuals alike must prioritize the security of these accounts to protect their assets and stop unauthorized access given the increased frequency of cyber dangers and fraud.From a business perspective, using strong security protocols to secure escrow accounts benefits both their reputation and dependability in addition to protecting the assets of their clients. Customers want assurance that their money is secure and that the escrow agent is taking all necessary precautions to prevent any fraudulent activity. Organizations may demonstrate their commitment to customer safety and build trust by implementing stringent security measures. This can increase customer loyalty and encourage repeat business.Customers who place money into an escrow account, however, also have a financial stake in keeping their possessions secure. They need to know that there are no flaws that might expose their assets to risks and that their money will only be released if the predetermined requirements are met. To ensure that the security measures in place meet their needs, clients should engage in active communication with the escrow agent.Here are some important things to think about to help businesses and people implement efficient security measures for escrow account protection:

1. Secure communication channels: To ensure that confidential information sent between parties is kept private and protected from being intercepted by unauthorized individuals, use encrypted communication channels, such as secure email or secure file transfer protocols.For instance, encrypting all correspondence about the escrow account—including account statements, transaction data, and private documents—from beginning to finish might significantly reduce the likelihood of data breaches.

2. Robust Access Restrictions: To restrict access to the escrow account system, use role-based access restrictions and multi-factor authentication (MFA). This reduces the risk of unauthorized access by guaranteeing that only authorized users may see or update account information.Example: Adding an extra degree of security to the account access procedure is the need that users submit a combination of something they know (password), something they have (security token), and something they are (biometric data) for authentication.

3. Frequent penetration tests and security audits: To find flaws in the escrow account system, do frequent penetration tests and security audits. This helps to prevent any invasions by proactively patching any flaws and implementing the necessary updates or patches.For instance, hiring a separate cybersecurity firm to do penetration testing might imitate actual attack situations and find any potential weaknesses in the system. This enables businesses to address these holes before malicious actors take advantage of them.

4. Ongoing Employee Training: Educate employees with access to the escrow account system about potential security risks, phishing scams, and the best ways to protect confidential data via in-depth training.Staff members might be the first line of defense against cyberattacks if regular training sessions and seminars are provided, covering topics like identifying phishing emails, creating strong passwords, and steering clear of unusual websites.

5. Consistent Account Monitoring: Put in place alert systems and real-time monitoring to spot any questionable activity or unauthorized access attempts. Early discovery might reduce the impact of any security flaws and help prevent any breaches. As an example, configuring automated alerts for any unusual account activity—like several failed login attempts or large money transfers—may encourage quick investigation and response, reducing the likelihood that fraudulent activity would go undetected.By implementing these stringent security measures, businesses and individuals may significantly increase the Putting of Sophisticated Escrow Account Management

Consistent observation and reconciliation of transactions in escrow accounts

Frequent Inspection

Effective escrow account management requires regular monitoring and reconciliation of escrow account transactions. The process involves a thorough analysis and cross-verification of all transactions inside the escrow account to ensure accuracy, compliance with relevant regulations, and adherence to contractual commitments. Financial institutions see this kind of monitoring as a way to confirm that the funds in the account are being used by the terms and conditions of the escrow agreement. It fosters a sense of security and confidence in the financial process by preserving transparency and trust amongst all stakeholders. On the other hand, monitoring and reconciliation provide reassurance to clients or parties placing money in escrow that their financial responsibilities are being managed appropriately and in the best interests of the deal.

1. Frequent reconciling of accounts

Comparing the transaction and balance records kept in the escrow account with those stated in the financial records is known as escrow account reconciliation. This process aids in identifying discrepancies, regardless of whether they stem from errors, fraudulent transactions, or other anomalies. Imagine, for example, a real estate transaction in which the buyer places funds for the purchase in an escrow account. Frequent reconciliation would ensure that money is efficiently used for property-related expenses, preventing misuse or misallocation.

2. Checking the Accuracy of Transactions

Transactions using escrow accounts must be accurate. Financial institutions may ensure that the monies disbursed or withdrawn precisely match the criteria outlined in the escrow agreement by closely examining each transaction. This fosters mutual trust amongst all parties and helps to avoid disputes. For example, thorough verification guarantees that the appropriate amounts are delivered to satisfy legitimate claims in a business transaction when money is held in escrow to cover potential liabilities.

3. Adherence to the law and regulatory requirements

In the financial sector, adherence to legal and regulatory requirements is essential. Escrow operations are governed by laws, and compliance with those laws may be checked by regularly monitoring and reconciling escrow account transactions. For example, if a healthcare organization sets up an escrow account to manage funds for supporting medical research, maintaining the institution's integrity and good name depends on compliance with fund use regulations.

4. Quick Discrepancy Identification and Resolution

Frequent monitoring facilitates the timely identification of discrepancies, allowing for swift action and resolution. It's critical to find a quick solution to maintain the integrity and confidence of the escrow process, regardless of whether the theft was intentional or the result of a clerical error. For instance, prompt settlement guarantees that a construction project moves forward without unnecessary delays if a dispute arises about the release of funds from an escrow account. In addition to adhering to strict financial guidelines, routine monitoring and reconciliation of escrow account transactions fosters reliability and a trustworthy environment. This crucial step serves as the foundation for effective escrow management by maintaining transparency, guaranteeing compliance, and swiftly addressing discrepancies.

Using Technology to Manage Escrow Accounts More Effectively

An increasingly important need in the dynamic and fast-paced financial industry of today is the efficient and straightforward management of escrow accounts. The management of escrow accounts requires a high degree of precision, transparency, and attention to detail to be financially successful. Thankfully, financial institutions and businesses today have access to a wide range of tools and platforms that may significantly increase the effectiveness and efficiency of managing escrow accounts thanks to the rapid advancements in technology.Financial organizations may find that using technology to manage escrow accounts significantly reduces the administrative burden that comes with manual processes. In the past, keeping an eye on escrow accounts required several laborious procedures, including reconciliation, document preparation, and manual data input. However, these tasks may now be decreased due to the emergence of automated systems and software, allowing financial institutions to focus on higher-value activities and provide better customer service.However, businesses that use escrow accounts might also benefit greatly from using technology. Organizations may easily monitor transactions, manage balances, and generate reports by using digital solutions that provide them with real-time access to information about their escrow accounts. This improves transparency and accountability in addition to increasing operational efficiency, which ultimately fosters trust between businesses and their partners or clients. To properly appreciate the potential benefits of using technology for the efficient management of escrow accounts, let's examine a few specific applications of technology:

1. Automated account reconciliation: By putting automated reconciliation processes in place, the time and effort required to match and confirm transactions may be significantly reduced. Organizations may automate the reconciliation process and ensure accuracy by integrating payment records, bank statements, and other pertinent data into a single system.A real estate company managing several escrow accounts, for instance, may use software that automatically associates money coming in and going out with the related transactions. In addition to saving time, this lowers the possibility of finding any discrepancies, ensuring that every account action is correctly recorded.

2. Technology provides a safe and effective way to manage and save important escrow account documents. This is known as secure document management. Organizations may provide quicker access, more collaboration, and improved security by using cloud-based storage solutions and digitizing documents. Imagine a global trade company that engages in escrow transactions regularly. The company may safely store and share important documents with relevant parties involved in the transaction by using a cloud-based document management system. Examples of these documents include purchase agreements, invoices, and shipping records. This eliminates the need for physical storage, lowers the possibility of losing documents,

and enables smooth communication across different places and time zones.

3. Interaction with Payment Systems: By combining escrow account management software with payment gateways, payment procedures are made more efficient and effective. Through the integration of the escrow account system with electronic money transfer or payment gateways, enterprises may reduce the need for human interaction by automating the distribution of cash. An e-commerce platform that uses escrow accounts, for example, may integrate its escrow account management system with well-known payment gateways to enable secure transactions. By eliminating the need for human review and approval of each transaction, this interface enables the automated disbursement of funds to vendors upon the buyer's confirmation of receipt of the goods.

4. Real-time reporting and analytics: Technology facilitates the creation of real-time data and the acquisition of significant insights on the operations of escrow accounts for enterprises. Organizations may improve their escrow account management approach by keeping an eye on transaction trends, seeing potential risks, and making informed decisions by using reporting and analytics technology. For instance, a financial institution that oversees many clients' escrow accounts may use analytics tools to look at transaction patterns and highlight any dubious activity.

Handling Legal and Regulatory Compliance in the Management of Escrow Accounts

The monitoring and administration of escrow accounts play a key role in the area of financial management by giving a mechanism to distribute and safeguard money for diverse reasons. Escrow accounts are commonly employed in real estate, business, and even legal transactions. But along with this growing dependency on escrow services comes the need to make sure that all legal and regulatory duties are followed, which may be a demanding and exhaustive endeavor. Let's analyze the challenges of maintaining legal and regulatory compliance in escrow account administration, taking into consideration opinions and offering useful guidance on this vital area of money management.

1. Being aware of the legal environment

Understanding the legal landscape is vital for managing escrow accounts and navigating compliance. The laws that apply to escrow accounts could change substantially depending on the jurisdiction and the specific cause of the escrow. For instance, the legal standards for escrow accounts in real estate transactions may be different from those in mergers and acquisitions. Learn about local, state, and federal laws, and chat with lawyers who concentrate on the subject area that interests you. There may be serious penalties and legal implications for breaching the law.

2. Select the Appropriate Financial Organization

It's crucial to find a suitable financial institution to handle your escrow account. Seek for firms that have a demonstrated track record of handling escrow accounts and a clear knowledge of the legal and regulatory environment. Do your homework and seek references to make sure the institution you chose is respected and compliant. You may decrease risks and keep within the law with the aid of a respected business.

3. Reporting and transparency

In handling escrow accounts, openness is key. As required by law, maintain detailed records of every transaction and make sure that everyone involved can examine them. You may stay away from any legal concerns and controversies by submitting correct and timely reports. For example, if you are in control of an escrow account in a real estate transaction, you may build trust amongst buyers, sellers, and agents by providing them with accurate information on the allocation of cash.

4. Safety Procedures

When maintaining an escrow account, security is vital. Put rigorous security measures in place to secure the money put in escrow. To defend against fraud or unauthorized access, utilize encryption, multi-factor authentication, and frequent audits. By doing this, you preserve your customers' trust in addition to abiding by the law.

Compliance with anti-money laundering (AML) and Know Your Customer (KYC)

Escrow accounts are typically deployed for large-scale financial transactions. Follow legislative obligations to develop KYC and AML processes to prevent financial crimes, including money laundering. Check the parties' identification and keep a watch out for any suspicious conduct during transactions. Neglecting these tasks may result in serious legal implications.

1. Respect for moral principles

While obeying the law is vital, preserving moral convictions may identify you as a trustworthy escrow account manager. Maintaining a high degree of knowledge, avoiding conflicts of interest, and treating all parties fairly are all components of ethical conduct. Over time, behaving ethically will not only keep you out of trouble with the police but also increase your status in the industry.

2. Ongoing Learning and Adjustment

The landscape of rules and regulations is dynamic and ever-changing. Keep up with any revisions to escrow account legislation so you can modify your operations. Participate in essential webinars, workshops, and seminars; additionally, sign up to receive regulatory bodies' mailings. Maintaining compliance involves being up to date. Escrow account management entails managing legal and regulatory compliance, which is a complicated endeavor that demands attention to detail and effort. You can successfully manage escrow accounts while minimizing legal risks by being aware of the legal landscape, selecting the best financial institution, emphasizing transparency, guaranteeing security, adhering to all KYC requirements, maintaining ethical standards, and keeping up with changing regulations.

Reducing Risks and Stopping Fraud in the Management of Escrow Accounts

Managing escrow accounts is vital to ensure the secure and effective transfer of money in a range of financial transactions. The employment of escrow accounts affords a level of protection for both buyers and sellers in real estate transactions, mergers and acquisitions, and other high-value transactions. Nonetheless, escrow account management includes significant hazards, just like any other financial operation. The integrity of escrow accounts may be jeopardized by dishonest conduct, money theft, and other hazards, which can result in substantial losses for all parties. To secure the money placed in escrow accounts, it is necessary to put suitable risk mitigation procedures and preventive measures into place.The primary function of the escrow agent is to ensure the protection and suitable management of the money entrusted to them. This requires carrying out rigorous due diligence on the parties of the transaction, validating the integrity of any supporting papers, and following stringent rules to stop any fraudulent behavior. To detect anomalies promptly, escrow agents must also maintain detailed records and reconcile the account periodically. Escrow agents may lessen the risk of fraud and preserve the money put in escrow by adopting a proactive posture and following best practices in managing escrow accounts. It is vital that the buyer carefully pick an established escrow service and thoroughly examine the terms and conditions of the escrow agreement. As an added precaution, purchasers should ensure that the escrow agency is authorized and subject to regulation by the appropriate authorities. To prevent falling for phishing or scam operations, customers should also exercise vigilance when validating the validity of the escrow account details that have been supplied to them, such as the beneficiary name and account number. Buyers may decrease their risk of fraud and ensure the security of their money by conducting their research and taking the initiative. In a similar vein, sellers should carefully assess their alternatives for an escrow agency and go over the provisions of the escrow agreement. Sellers must maintain a strict check on the transaction's progress and tell the escrow agent immediately once of any suspicious activities or abnormalities. Furthermore, requests for modifications to the escrow account details or unforeseen delays in the receipt of money might raise red flags for sellers. Sellers may lessen the risks associated with operating an escrow account and preserve their financial interests by paying strict attention to detail and adopting proactive actions.

Here are some suggested procedures to take into consideration to increase security and decrease risks related to maintaining escrow accounts:

1. Exercise meticulous due diligence: Before selecting an escrow agent, check into their background to make sure they are trustworthy and that the necessary authorities have issued them a license and regulation.

2.Put multi-factor authentication into practice: Make sure that only authorized personnel can access the escrow account by utilizing strong authentication mechanisms like biometrics or token-based authentication.

3. Regularly reconcile accounts: To swiftly uncover any inconsistencies or illicit activity, undertake routine reconciliations.

4. Educate everyone concerned: To increase the awareness of probable dangers and preventive measures, buyers, sellers, and escrow agents should get complete training and instructional resources.

5. Put in place comprehensive internal controls Escrow officers should set up tight norms and methods for handling money, such as internal reporting systems, periodic audits, and work segregation.

6. Keep up with technology: To increase the security and transparency of escrow account management, make use of cutting-edge technologies like blockchain or secure cloud-based platforms.

7. Keep an eye out for warning signs: Put in place dependable monitoring systems to identify dubious behavior, such as rapid changes in transaction patterns or unusual delays in money transfers.

Stakeholders in escrow may take a proactive approach and employ these best practices.

Constant Modification and Enhancement of Escrow Account Management Procedures

Enhancement and Modification Constant Modification and Enhancement Success in any job, including escrow account administration, is primarily contingent on constant adaptation and progress in account management. Escrow professionals need to be on top of developments in the financial sector and make sure that their procedures are current and comply with industry best practices. Escrow account managers may boost their effectiveness and efficiency, and ultimately the financial success of their clients, by adopting a mindset that stresses ongoing adaptation and growth. The client's opinion should be taken into consideration when talking about continual adaptation and development in escrow account management. From the client's standpoint, escrow accounts are the safest location to hold and manage their assets. They expect that the manager of their escrow account will have solid processes in place to secure their assets and ensure transparency in all interactions. Escrow account managers may supply their clients piece of mind by continually boosting their processes, guaranteeing that their money is being managed cautiously and reliably.From the viewpoint of the escrow account manager, industry competitiveness relies on constant innovation and adaptation. Escrow professionals have to adapt to new tools and methods that can boost their productivity and optimize their operations as rules change and technology improves. Implementing automated escrow management software, for instance, may boost productivity, cut down on human errors, and give real-time visibility into account activities. Escrow account managers may make sure they are giving their clients the finest possible service by continually reacting to new technology breakthroughs and industry trends.Let's now review some specific strategies that may help escrow account management's continuing evolution and adaptability:

1. Keep up with regulatory changes and industry trends

Escrow professionals should actively seek information about best practices, new regulations, and industry advancements. Attending conferences, taking part in webinars, and keeping relationships with professional networks are methods to achieve this. Escrow account managers may proactively adapt their practices to accommodate changing client needs and regulatory requirements by becoming trained.

2. Often evaluate and update internal procedures

To uncover possibilities for improvement, escrow account managers should examine and update their internal processes often. This can involve carrying out frequent audits to assure compliance, improving processes to enhance efficiency, or putting in place additional security measures to secure client money. Professionals working with escrow may expedite their operations and boost client satisfaction by frequently analyzing and improving internal processes.

3. Adopt technical solutions

Modern escrow account management methods are considerably facilitated by technology. Escrow account managers must study and deploy technology solutions that automate repetitive labor, streamline operations, and offer quick reporting. For example, secure online portals may increase communication and document exchange with clients, while electronic signature platforms may speed up the signing process and decrease paperwork. Adopting technology solutions may raise productivity and increase consumer contentment in general.

4. Ask for consumer input

Constantly asking for client feedback is a wonderful strategy to acquire information for continuing improvement. Managers of escrow accounts should actively seek out feedback via meetings, surveys, and informal discussions. This feedback may aid in discovering new consumer needs, indicating opportunities for improvement, and boosting the client relationship overall. Escrow account managers may continuously adapt their methods to better serve their customers by paying attention to what their clients have to say and making the appropriate modifications.

5. Invest in professional growth

Investing in one's professional development is another part of constant improvement. Professionals in escrow should actively explore methods to expand their knowledge and experience by enrolling in courses, gaining certifications, or engaging in training programs. Escrow account managers may expand their expertise and give value to their clients by acquiring new skills and keeping up with industry changes.

Chapter 6

THE CHANGE IN REAL ESTATE DIGITAL MARKETING

This is the right opportunity to boost your internet presence. Create a strategy for your internet marketing approach by strengthening your brand values, finding out how to represent them, and amassing a ton of social evidence.Real estate is becoming a more digital business. Our present position is not indicative of where we will be in a decade. Professionals must not simply stay up with growing digital products, but also with how real estate digital marketing is evolving. Staying ahead of the competition and getting equipped for the new realities of the digital real estate sector entails adopting the newest advancements and trends. We've been studying marketing trends and have uncovered a few aspects that the real estate industry should begin implementing into its strategic approach.

Voice Recognition

Do you believe Siri or Alexa have no utility in your real estate company? Rethink your ideas. You should examine how voice search could locate you if you are selling any form of products or services.

In 2023, voice search accounted for roughly 40% of all browsing sessions, according to one research. Voice search is used every day by 41% of users to discover local firms, including real estate services. A voice search for real estate may be beneficial in a few different ways. It has to do with location-based services in part. Voice search is widely used by users to locate goods surrounding their current location.If they have heard about you from someone, they might potentially be seeking you expressly via your name. Possibly all they can remember about your firm is the last name, such as **"Pullis Real Estate."**

Will your listing show in their search results?

Another way it works is that a user may ask for the top real estate agents in their city by utilizing a voice search. The best-rated Google business profiles or Yelp profiles are utilized to build the voice search results. This is simply another rationale for continuing to urge your customers for as many five-star reviews as you can.

What activities are essential for you to profit from voice search?

Make sure your current firm address is updated on all of your online accounts, including your Google business profile, before continuing. We are aware that real estate agents typically have vast workstations and that your actual brokerage address may not be near your primary place of business. To guarantee that your voice search results stand up in your local area, at least offer a partial home address.

Make sure your website's keywords and all of your profiles are optimized for particular phrases. Incorporate the keywords into all of your business profiles and online marketing so that people will still notice you even if they can't recollect your complete name. When writing, take in mind how people speak. Asking a query via SMS is not the same as asking Cortana or Siri. Where is the closest burger restaurant near me? is the inquiry we would ask Alexa instead of putting in "best burger bar in

Polaris." In the following years, more residences will have voice search devices and smart speakers installed. Optimize for voice search to boost the discoverability of your organization.

Adoption of virtual reality

Look, you should be acquainted with virtual and augmented reality by now if you work in the real estate sector. It's realistic to predict that by 2025, virtual tours will be an integral feature of any marketing campaign.The availability of VR and AR technology will only rise. Many firms give interactive 3D models and building tours so that consumers may properly check the item or the property well in advance. VR technology saves customers time and money by enabling them to narrow down their selection of homes without having to physically see them.Real estate agents may produce virtual tours of homes using several approaches. Project management and construction product documentation may both benefit from these related technologies. Moreover, virtual and augmented reality are being utilized by designers and architects to minimize the number of errors made during building. Before the first piece of earth is taken, the technology enables builders to explain new construction concepts to the buyer's wants.We've already seen how commercial and residential spaces are sold utilizing virtual tours. But purchases aren't restricted to homes. Extend to include virtual tours of a community or neighborhood to provide prospective residents a feel of the region they may be living in.Large stores such as Amazon and IKEA employ augmented reality to help buyers see how the things and furnishings they purchase will look in a given region. Real estate brokerages also use it to illustrate how a property may be refurbished or to evaluate whether a client's furniture will fit in the region they are contemplating buying. Be innovative with your virtual marketing to anticipate greater usage of virtual tours. This is being referred to as the **"Spatial Web" or "Web 3.0"** by some. It involves the seamless movement from the actual world to the virtual and vice versa.

Expansion of social media advertisements

To be the next big thing, keep an eye out for freshly built social networking sites.A notable example is the **Clubhouse app,** a creative way of networking that blends the ephemeral aspects of Snapchat or Instagram Stories with podcasts, webinars, and conferences. Though it is still in beta as of this writing, it is fast gaining popularity as the next "it" social networking site. You may have live, audio chats with industry pros about several issues by utilizing the Clubhouse app. After enquiring about your areas of interest upon registration, it presents you with a selection of persons you may find fascinating to follow. There aren't any videos, images, or status updates of any type. You talk into your phone to begin a chatroom. What is mentioned in your chat room is audible to everyone. You extend your hand to alert the moderators and join the debate. You may work directly with other real estate industry influencers in many of the specialized chat rooms.Any new social media network will experiment with advertising. Thus, remain aware of trends in the social media sector. Always explore how you can employ a platform to boost the awareness of your brand and how you can use its advertising reach to strengthen your sales funnel.

Growth of one's brand

It's becoming extremely clear that real estate brokers put a great emphasis on branding. In addition to individual real estate agents, service providers like escrow businesses and insurance organizations also require a recognized brand.Business progress will be noticed by real estate professionals who construct significant real estate brands.It goes beyond merely having a website and a logo when we consider branding. They want to make sure that the people they're using to manage all of their real estate needs are dependable. Creating seamless digital and real-world experiences is the first step toward creating that trust. The purpose of personal branding is to make the business of real estate more accessible. Storytelling and conveying brand values will be crucial components of personal branding in the future. Social issues are a worry for individuals. They would rather do business with individuals who share their beliefs and are willing to take a stand. A detailed branding strategy that defines everything from the purpose to the brand promise is crucial for all real estate brokers. It will still contain the website and visual components like colors, fonts, and logos.

The target market and brand values must also be explored.Develop a unified brand strategy for all marketing assets, including printed and digital. Regardless of the age of your real estate firm, branding is vital to its success.

Marketing Targeting Millennials

Without addressing the millennial generation, it is hard to establish strategies for the future of the real estate business. They are the top candidates for the following years. Two groups sometimes make up the millennial generation. Millennials who were born between 1980 and 1989 are commonly referred to as **Generation Z** or the **elder generation**. Millennials who are younger were born between 1990 and 1998. Presently, elder millennials account for 36% of housing purchases, with younger millennials accounting for 15%. But this is simply the tip of the iceberg. The capacity of millennials to acquire property has been hindered by various social and economic challenges. They are currently at the point where they are prepared and ready to invest in real estate. Now is the optimum opportunity to boost the amount of attention you give to millennial marketing.Start by engaging in areas where millennials are active. The possibility is that they will discover you online. This means leveraging social media and the Internet as part of a comprehensive digital strategy. Once again, you should keep a watch on the rise of social media advertisements and the arrival of new social media platforms. To gain the attention of millennials, build a presence on the platforms they frequent. However, be aware that millennials dislike direct sales approaches. They will prefer to associate with firms and persons who share their ideals. They will want to start a chat with you first. Once again, having a great brand will aid in this case. Social proof is more essential to millennials than direct marketing. This generation was raised with the ability to speak their thoughts, engage in discourse, and put in two cents. They will be searching for social proof or indication that other partners have approved of your work. Accumulating as many 5-star reviews as you can is important to your business's future success. Create a strategy for your internet marketing approach by strengthening your brand values, finding out how to represent them, and amassing a ton of social evidence.

Modifications to marketing targeting

If you've been in the real estate marketing field for a while, you've seen some changes in the ways that we target our audiences on social media and other platforms. In the past, we used to target people more accurately when running adverts. For example, age-based targeting for real estate marketing is no longer allowed. This tendency of lowering audience targeting specificity may expand to other ad networks. That does not stop us from concentrating on our target audiences, however. It simply suggests that our method of reaching the persons we need to reach will need to be altered.This suggests, in part, that we must strengthen our behavior-based audience targeting strategies. Currently, we may concentrate on a broad keyword like **"Lexington real estate"** and segment the audience into those persons who appear to be interested in buying or selling based on their recent online behavior. Google ad campaigns are already benefiting from this in terms of increased targeting. For the real estate industry, behavior-based targeting may deliver a greater return on investment. Ultimately, not everyone is constantly seeking to acquire or sell a property and employ the accompanying services. It can be years before they require the services of a real estate agent.Their search activity shows they are a wonderful match for your behavior-based marketing when they do start to demonstrate interest.

Marketing And Video

To interact with customers and create a brand, video marketing is vital because, Videos have greater interest.You may express your brand personality with videos. When learning something, individuals are more inclined to watch a video than to read about it. When we see and hear about something, we are more likely to remember it than when we merely read about it.Videos perform effectively on several social networking platforms, including LinkedIn, Instagram, and YouTube.The benefit of video marketing is that it doesn't have to be elaborate or long. Why do you suppose social networking networks that offer you 60 seconds, like TikTok, are so popular? The length of the most watched videos is normally two minutes, however, the perfect duration may vary greatly based on the platform and objective of the video.People are more engaged with live videos than they are with ordinary videos. People keep tuned in because they worry they'll miss some important news, or what's known as the **"fear of missing out."** You may reach a bigger audience with videos as you may tag the folks who are featured. They are also highly adaptive. Use videos to perform live property tours in real estate, give homeowners 60-second suggestions, organize a thorough webinar on financing with a mortgage lender partner, and much more. Digital marketing for real estate will rely more and more on video marketing.

Bots on your site

Likely, you have already utilized a chatbot for customer assistance. It's time to move beyond the fundamental inquiries that chatbots react to. An excellent marketing tool for creating a connection with potential customers is a chatbot.A website bot can differentiate between a user who is merely looking and someone who is actively seeking to buy or sell. You must become skilled with this chatbot for your website since lead generation will rely on it. A well-designed bot starts by communicating with the user and asking some introductory queries. It identifies their search phrases and the reason they arrived at your website. What follows next—the chatbot delivers the visitor with personalized marketing content—is the genuine goldmine. For instance, the bot might question, "Do you want a free market analysis for Haines City? "if it ascertains that the user is on the website to acquire a property in a given location."By giving the consumer these important items, you may gain their contact information, create a connection with them, and ultimately convert them into a client. Chatbots will be a terrific digital marketing tool as a consequence,

Virtual Real Estate Gold

The future of digital marketing for real estate. The newest technology must be acquainted with everyone who works in the real estate sector. Our use of technology expands the range of services we can provide and boosts marketing ROI. When it comes to digital marketing for real estate, our approach is developing into something more interesting and customer-focused than it has ever been.

Chapter 7

Targeted Advertising

An Easy Way to Connect with Your Audience

When applied successfully, ad targeting may help pull in new customers, maintain hold of present ones, and improve knowledge of your firm. This is the procedure.

Targeted advertising

What is it?

Targeted advertising develops and distributes commercials that are targeted to the interests of the user based on information obtained about them, including demographics, browsing patterns, and website interactions.

Where Can Targeted Ads Be Published?

There are various techniques open to businesses for releasing personalized adverts. Email is a superb technique to target consumers who are already interested in your organization with advertising provided they have opted-in to get newsletters and offers. Meanwhile, businesses may buy personalized advertising to show on social media platforms like Facebook, Instagram, or TikTok to reach a wider audience. Additional alternatives include presenting targeted adverts via the Google display network, which covers 90% of worldwide Internet users, or in customers' Google search results. Both are managed by an auction system and are included in the wider category of Google Ads. Marketers submit the greatest cost per click they are willing to pay for advertising, and Google utilizes the maximum bid and overall ad quality to calculate the position and price of the ad. Important to note? Only when a consumer clicks through on your link will brands be billed. So, how can you utilize ad targeting to help your company? Boost the impact of your adverts with these 10 suggested tactics.

Best Practices for Ad Targeting

Targeted advertising develops and distributes commercials that are targeted to the interests of the user based on information obtained about them, including demographics, browsing patterns, and website interactions.

1. Provide Customers with Relevant Content

Use customized adverts as a technique to supply customers with new information and offers that they would find interesting based on their prior browsing and purchase behavior, rather than telling them what they already know. Show your customers that you respect their company by presenting them with information that is especially targeted to what they would want to see in advertising.The conclusion is that viewers desire original, fresh stuff so give them the best.

2. Maintain Interest

Marketing is supposed to be **"creative"** as it needs to be intriguing, active, and anything but boring. Given that commercials are frequently overlooked, a targeted ad must be exceedingly conspicuous to be successful. The key is to make your adverts striking.

3. Place a Cap on the Wavelength

It's crucial to bear in mind that whereas smart ad targeting ought to aid your customers, excessive utilization of it will probably have the contrary effect. From the viewpoint of a client, think how angry you would be if you saw the same advertising on hundreds of different websites all the time. The lesson is, Don't bombard your client with advertising.

4. Locate the Appropriate Location

Not every platform is where your advertising should be put. While easy and uncomplicated advertising makes sense for Google search results, it's worthwhile taking the effort to design more intricate ads for Facebook or Instagram marketing campaigns. When consumers see your ad, they're more likely to click over to a new page or view a video rather than continuing to browse. The lesson is that location, location, location is vital for effective ad targeting, just as it is for real estate.

5. Determine Who Your Audience Is

Identifying your target demographic is vital to any targeted advertising strategy. You won't obtain the click-through rates you desire if you're giving them ads that don't meet their preferences. It's vital to undertake extensive research to develop tailored adverts based on specific customer data and to acquire a better knowledge of your target by uncovering common traits. The improper audience won't react to even the finest commercial ads, so make sure you target the right Audience.

6. Avoid being overly detailed

Conversely, it's vital to guarantee that your adverts reach a sufficient number of your desired audience. An advertisement that targets, for instance, redheaded men in Kansas between the ages of 20 and 22 who drive electric cars, own golden retrievers, and are specifically targeted would be extremely specific, so much so that it is unlikely to appear in many social media or search feeds and to garner a sizable enough audience share.The lesson learned is that smart marketing avoids going too far in one way with its targeting.

7. Consider Alternative Approaches

Developing a concentrated advertising campaign includes evaluating the demands of your target market. Assume you run a real estate business and help individuals in purchasing or selling their current dwellings. People browsing for local realtors or comparing property prices in their communities are your target market. However, it's also crucial to take into consideration relevant secondary markets to your core purpose. In the context of real estate, this may entail searching for moving boxes, hiring a truck or van, or seeking storage lockers, all of which might be signals that a client is getting ready to migrate. Expanding your reach without losing focus may be done by going beyond traditional thinking and investigating parallel markets. The lesson gained is that both breadths of interest and depth of customization are important for targeted marketing.

8. Test it out

The best-laid strategies for advertising don't always work out. Because of this, it's necessary to periodically undertake A/B testing to establish which adverts outperform others in particular conditions and which lags. After establishing the front-runners, you may optimize them further by consistently running A/B testing to gain the maximum return on investment.

The lesson: Nothing is perfect the first time. To make your ads function better, test them.

9. Cast a Broad Net

A new advertising campaign will likely work well on one advertising platform. The warning? You must try them all to discover which is your favorite. It's important to experiment with new ad platforms to learn what works, even if it's not worth utilizing your complete advertising budget to flood the Internet with fresh marketing activities.

The lesson: You may identify where your clients are swimming with broad nets and change your methods appropriately.

10. Calculate Your Effect

Everything should go according to plan if clicks are happening and advertising is being seen, right? Perhaps, perhaps not. It's necessary to develop critical performance indicators and regularly evaluate them to make sure concentrated advertising campaigns are providing the expected outcomes. To evaluate whether the statistics make up, you may, for instance, compare the total value of conversions to the expenditure of a concentrated marketing campaign.The lesson is to monitor the statistics to verify that advertising expenditures are justified.

How to Organize a Profitable Online Open House in 2024 and Get Leads

Open houses have naturally adapted to the digital age as real estate has. Zillow observed a nearly 200% spike in virtual open-house experiences in the first weeks of March 2020, coinciding with the COVID-19 pandemic. This signified a huge growth in virtual interactions. Virtual open houses are still well-liked by buyers even as the real estate market decreases from all-time highs. 97% of buyers of real estate are estimated to browse online for their future property. This online experience includes virtual open houses, which enable consumers to explore homes without getting off the couch. You enhance the amount of probable leads in your market by conducting a virtual open house. If a buyer enjoys your transparency and presentation of a home, they may follow you on social media or subscribe to updates on your website even if they aren't ready to make an offer on your listing.

When should you host a virtual open house and what does it entail?

In contrast to looking at images or descriptions, a virtual open house is an online experience that provides potential buyers with a greater knowledge of a home or property. A real estate agent guides prospective buyers around a home in real-time, answering questions and delivering an interactive tour of the property. These tours are commonly performed via video conferencing systems. Despite being necessary during COVID-19, virtual open houses have demonstrated to be quite robust. They are especially beneficial in the following situations:

❖ Buyers from out-of-state or faraway regions exhibit a tremendous degree of interest in a property. When showing a house, a real estate agent prefers to organize group showings over individual ones. The seller would want less foot traffic during the selling process as they still live and work at their house. For a property that receives a lot of online traffic, virtual open houses are a terrific approach to developing leads. It helps convert searchers into serious shoppers and gives a less intrusive technique to promote a home's outstanding characteristics.

How to get ready for the online open house

A small bit of planning ahead of time might pay significant returns when it comes to your virtual open house. Before the big day, remember to take these vital steps:

1. Select the platform.

Before anything else, you must pick a place for your online open house. Different platforms give distinct features that could enhance your event.

Zoom: This is a well-liked choice if you want something basic and lively. You may host dozens of people, share your screen, and even record the session for later use.

Facebook Live and Instagram Live: These platforms enable you to communicate with your followers on social media in a more casual way. Additionally, you will be able to view your open house video again on your feed.

Platforms like Matterport or other 3D tour providers: If you want to completely immerse yourself in the virtual environment, these providers give 3D tours that enable customers to "walk through" the property at their leisure. Keep in mind that your selection should take your target audience's degree of technical knowledge into consideration.

2. Arrange the flow

After picking your platform, carefully evaluate the flow so that you know what facts to present, the characteristics of the property to emphasize, and the route you'll follow to take visitors on a virtual tour of the house. Depending on the size and attributes of the property, a superb virtual tour frequently lasts between 10 and 20 minutes. Making the most of your potential buyer's time and being prepared is vital as this may be your last chance to show the home to them. You may even consider making a day out of a virtual session. Set up a complete day to organize events for every listing you have. Encourage potential buyers to come and view a home being showcased by marketing them. Give the home's staging the same attention and consideration as you would an in-person open house. Think about virtual staging, which enhances your home's finest characteristics by decorating it with new furniture and décor. A less intrusive (and less expensive) approach is to digitally stage the property, which entails utilizing software to construct an image of what the house might seem like for possible buyers.

To make sure you hit the highlights during the virtual open house, develop a list of discussion topics for viewers. Together with your staff, build a system of duties to preserve order, especially if you're not the only one showing off the property. Lastly, execute a test run with your group to gain advice on the optimum staging, lighting, and camera angles for a virtual environment.

3. Spread the word about your online open house.
The listing, email blasts to your network and other agents, social media postings, and advertising campaigns are some of the ways you may market your event. Provide plenty of facts and

attention-grabbing high-quality images of the property, along with information on when and how to attend the virtual open house. Seek their support in promoting the event if you're hiring luxury real estate marketing services to reach as many possible buyers as you can.

How to handle oneself during the virtual open house

Using a hand-held phone to shoot video during a virtual open house

When the time comes to conduct the virtual open house and you've prepared, you'll want to make sure everything goes as planned and leaves an impression on your visitors. Here's how to create an impact during the important event:

1. Establish the scene

Begin by expressing a warm welcome to all attendees and detailing the program of activities for the open house. Give them a quick summary of the property and the virtual tour's timetable. Informing attendees of the right time and technique for asking questions—for example, whether a Q&A will follow the event or whether they should simply provide questions in the chat window as they come to mind—is also important.

2. Offer a guided tour

It's showtime now! Give a guided tour of the location to your visitors. Don't forget to underline the property's biggest characteristics and special selling propositions. With a 3D virtual tour platform, you can walk visitors around the room while giving feedback. Make sure the video is stable and clear while you walk around the property if you wish to go live.

3. Engage in discussion

Encourage interaction from attendees throughout the event. To keep things interesting, obtain their comments on the property or share intriguing details about the neighborhood or house's background.

Additionally, bear in mind to regularly watch the chat and address any questions or comments that emerge.

4. Respond to queries

Allow time to address any questions or comments that visitors may have following the tour. This is your opportunity to add further information on the property, the purchase method, or any other essential data. Being honest and educated boosts your credibility and may put potential consumers at rest.

5. Conclude with the following activities

Inform visitors of the following activities to take if they are interested in the property after the event. This can include offering information on how to make an offer or arranging for private online or in-person showings. Remember to show thanks to everyone for their time and leave your contact information in case there are any additional inquiries.

6. Remain composed and optimistic.

Keep a pleasant but professional way during the full virtual open house. Recall that in addition to selling the property, you are showcasing your expertise and talents in delivering client service. Remain optimistic even if there are technology challenges (which could happen with virtual meetings!). Your aptitude for seamless problem-solving may have a major influence. These ideas will help you organize a virtual open house that highlights your abilities as a digital-age real estate agent while also being instructive and enjoyable.

Invest in a luxury presence to strengthen your real estate brand.

Entering the domain of digital open houses is merely the start. It is your obligation as a real estate agent to make sure that every digital touchpoint, virtual tour, and interaction matches your brand. Luxury Presence is ready to help.We are aware that real estate is about more than just acquiring and selling properties; it's also about offering your consumers an experience they won't soon forget. We can help you build your online presence, boost your customer base, and improve your brand with our website design and digital marketing services. Get started with a live demo right now if you're prepared to stand out from the competition.

How To Write Attractive Real Estate Listings

Creating an appealing property listing is vital in the real estate market. You may fast-sell properties and pull in potential purchasers with a well-written property listing. While most people don't think much of real estate listings, appealing and intriguing listings are vital for pulling in prospective buyers.

Consumer behavior has shifted as a consequence of the internet's introduction and extensive availability internationally. Now, consumers prefer to explore things online before making an immediate buy. Properties in real estate are no different. Therefore, to pull in purchasers, emphasize the home's particular traits, and develop an emotional connection with them, it is vital to write appealing and fascinating property descriptions. Today, we'll go over a few practical tactics and ideas that might help you develop appealing and fascinating real estate listings.

Recognize Your Goal Audience

When establishing a real estate listing, you should keep potential buyers in mind as you are seeking to convince them to purchase a house. A competitive real estate listing needs to understand who your target market is. To build an attractive real estate listing, you should analyze the target audience's demographics, needs, preferences, pain points, and reasons. Then, you should alter your listing to appeal to each of these categories. For example, you will need to develop a distinct listing for first-time homeowners than you would for luxury property investors. Consequently, you may build a listing that will appeal to your target audience by undertaking market research to acquire insights into your target audience and their buying behaviors.

Determine and Emphasize the Main Selling Elements

Make sure to attract attention to the primary selling characteristics of your house while crafting a listing. To fascinate and lure consumers in any industry, it is vital to stress distinctive selling traits. Even well-known organizations like Marriott highlight their unique selling propositions as doing so is crucial to pulling in clientele.Determine the particular traits and benefits of the property you are presenting, such as its beautiful view, huge backyard, historic importance, etc. Once you've discovered these crucial selling points, make sure to present them in the listing to attract the reader's attention straight away. Use narrative strategies to produce powerful sentiments in the reader's brain that will urge them to acquire the piece of real estate.

Compose an Interesting Property Description

You should be able to lure the reader into your property listing with a dynamic headline and an opening comment that piques the reader's interest in the property description. It is crucial to create an appealing headline that piques readers' curiosity while correctly describing the property. To persuade the reader to keep reading, the introductory sentence should offer a brief overview of the property. Try to keep the rest of the description short and instructive. To make things easy for the reader, you may utilize bullet points or concise paragraphs. Large text additions should be avoided as they may overwhelm and turn off potential clients. Make sure you utilize your words to assist readers imagine the hotel and develop a sense of connection. To further boost the description's readability, underline all the distinctive traits and conveniences.

Add Top-Notch Illustrations

Adding top-notch photos is vital to bringing in clients in addition to other things. Make sure you include high-resolution images in your listing to showcase the distinctive features, layout, and mood of the house. This will make it more competitive and exciting. If you're not excellent with photography, you may engage a professional to create gorgeous images that show off the property to its fullest advantage. In addition to images, you may consider incorporating videos and virtual tours of the property so that prospective buyers can view it all from the comfort of their own homes. Buyers have a unique chance to demonstrate the flow and layout of the property utilizing virtual tours.

Arrange the Listing

Finally, to assist navigation, correctly and logically organize the listing. Use headers, subheadings, and bullet points to make the listing easy for readers to browse and contain all important information. It will be easier for clients to access the information they need if it is presented nicely.

Property Regulation in the Metaverse

Being researched every day. Even while the notion is attractive and a lot is going on, the field is still very flexible. Individuals are still straining to properly appreciate what it is. To put it another way, it's a continually developing field. It's exciting to learn about themes like augmented reality, virtual reality, blockchain technology, and cryptocurrency. It's tough to resist the desire to get engaged in what sounds like an exciting and maybe successful endeavor. Moreover, obtaining NFTs and bitcoin is growing popular and attracting a lot of attention. You hear stories of billionaires and celebrities investing in NFTs, cryptocurrencies, and metaverse real estate everyday. What's the significance of it all? If you are not engaged in the IT field, it may be quite complex and scary. This section gives a comprehensive summary of the present condition of real estate law in the metaverse, even if it does not include everything that is happening in the metaverse—or maybe we should say, metaverse—world. So to get a feel of what to expect from real estate law in the metaverse, continue reading.

What is meant by the Metaverse?

There are multiple Metaverses; there isn't just "one." The most well-known and well-liked metaverses are Sandbox, Illuvium, and Decentraland. When individuals allude to the **"metaverse,"** they frequently merely mean the internet, **virtual reality, or augmented reality.** The phrase "metaverse" is overused and there is no one form of metaverse. The creation of numerous metaverses may be utilized to identify them from one another. Blockchain technology or so-called "off-chain" technologies may serve as the basis for a metaverse.Blockchain technology: public, private, hybrid, and consortium are the four types of blockchain technology. We will stick to the core definition of blockchain for this section, which is an immutable, shared ledger that registers transactions like the exchange of physical and immaterial things. Things like autos and real estate are examples of physical assets. Intellectual property and patents are examples of intangible assets. Information on the shared ledger is supposed to be more secure as it cannot be changed. Blockchain ensures quicker and more trustworthy information transmission, minimizing risk and eventually saving money for all stakeholders.

Distinctive Technology

Virtual Real Estate Gold

It's easy to grasp; this refers to any transaction that doesn't happen on the blockchain. Usually, a third party fills the role of guarantor, ensuring the transaction. A video game that is produced and then sold to consumers would be an example of an off-chain technology-based metaverse. A blockchain metaverse may be likened to a platform for virtual reality that a human might access with computer aid and experience as either augmented or virtual reality. Now that cryptocurrencies are a reality, you can purchase digital products and "real estate" in a blockchain metaverse. The space "inside" a metaverse is split into numerous pieces that are for sale. To put it another way, real estate is split into lots and parts. Real estate purchases are made using cryptocurrencies, so before trying to begin and invest in metaverse real estate—a subject this book section will not address is that you must know cryptocurrencies, because that's the foundation of investing in real estate Metaverse.Information on real estate purchases made in the metaverse is encoded into a "non-fungible token."

Non-transferable Token

In blockchain technology, a non-fungible token, or NFT, is a cryptographic asset. An NFT may be identified from other NFTs by their unique identification code and other information. Metadata, to the layperson, is information that describes other information. They can't be traded, and it doesn't appear like they can be created either. NFTs may be likened to cryptocurrencies. Every cryptocurrency has a similar "look"; for example, every Bitcoin is identical to every other Bitcoin, however, every NFT is unique. This is a fraction of the extra safety that blockchain technology gives to individuals who deal with exceptionally secure, quick, and accurate information. Upon obtaining real estate within the metaverse, you will possess your NFT, which acts as a documentation of your ownership of that particular metaverse location. Your NFT will work within that metaverse in the same way that a real estate deed would in the actual world.

In the Metaverse, Where Does Real Estate Law Fit?

After obtaining your virtual reality property and getting your **"deed"** from your NFT, what legal restrictions apply to your newly acquired virtual property?

Rights of Ownership

This implies that you are now entirely in charge of that virtual reality asset, and you may dispose of it just like you would any other real estate in this world. You are free to develop it, sell it, rent it out, or do nothing at all. It is wholly yours, much like having a big tract of land in the real world.

It's Possible to Grow Your Virtual Property

The newest trend includes purchasing land in a metaverse, acquiring an NFT, and then developing it for events, commercial usage (such as virtual storefronts), or advertising (such as leasing the area to a virtual billboard). Put another way, it may be highly advantageous to own real estate in the metaverse. The demand for metaverse real estate has escalated to the point where financing, like a mortgage, is now available for virtual transactions. Zoning restrictions don't appear to apply to real estate in the metaverse, so you can make your property commercial—and you definitely should, given the profit possibilities.

You Can Purchase Something with a Mortgage and Face Foreclosure

You can receive money to purchase real estate in a metaverse, just as you do in the actual world. The firm will lend you the bitcoin to purchase the real estate, with your NFT acting as collateral. Until the loan is repaid, the lender will potentially control your NFT, just as they would with real land. The lender can foreclose on the debt by pressing a button if the borrower fails. The NFT will be transferred from the escrow account into the lender's virtual wallet during the "foreclosure." As of right present, there is no judicial foreclosure. The main advantage is that you are still living in your home and are not facing eviction, even if there may be more involved foreclosure proceedings in the future. For now, however, it's as easy as pressing a button. However, a virtual property mortgage is still a legal transaction, so you should check with a lawyer before signing anything. That's real estate law in the current metaverse. Since this is still a relatively young and expanding sector, additional restrictions limiting how a party may utilize their section of the virtual world may be in place in a year. This is an exciting period for technology, and new metaverses with transferable virtual properties are expected to arise.

Getting Around Real Estate Contract Drafting and Negotiations

Real estate transactions demand meticulous attention to detail owing to the numerous technical rules and intricacies involved. Negotiation and drafting of contracts is a vital phase in the real estate transaction. These occupations require expertise, precision, and a profound awareness of the regulations regulating real estate transactions. This article will cover the necessity of efficient contract negotiations and drafting in real estate, go over significant variables to consider, and underline the benefits of seeking experienced support at this vital moment.

How Important Are Contract Negotiations?

The bedrock of a successful transaction is real estate contract negotiations. The parties participating in these negotiations, which include buyers, sellers, brokers, and attorneys, must negotiate and reach compromises.Finding mutually beneficial agreements that secure each party's interests is the fundamental objective. During conversations, it's crucial to keep the purchase price, financing conditions, timeframes, contingencies, and probable conflicts in mind.

Efficient Drafting for Protection and Clarity

The next step after the bargaining process is finished is to construct a detailed and legally strong contract. Real estate contracts are fairly complicated legal agreements that describe each party's rights, obligations, and responsibilities. Drafting aims to eliminate ambiguity, define the terms and conditions of the agreement, and lessen the possibility of future disagreements.

Important Things to Keep in Mind When Drafting Real Estate Contracts

Precise Identification of Parties: All parties, including buyers, sellers, agents, and any other relevant stakeholders, should be accurately named in the contract. Enforceability and confusion avoidance are guaranteed by explicit identification.

Terms and Property Description: It is vital to offer a complete and accurate description of the property, including its boundaries, structures, and other facilities that may be present. Furthermore, criteria concerning the purchase price, forms of payment, finance arrangements, and eventualities must be included.

Contingencies and Due Diligence: Any contingencies, including financing, title searches, property inspections, and appraisals, should be stated in the contract. Before closing the transaction, the parties may undertake due diligence owing to these contingencies.

Legal Compliance and Disclosures: Local, state, and federal laws must be adhered to in real estate transactions. Include any applicable disclosures, including those concerning lead-based paint, zoning requirements, and any known faults or essential facts about the property.

Dispute Resolution and Remedies

To address any disagreements, the contract should contain dispute resolution mechanisms like arbitration or mediation. It should also define the proper remedies—such as specific performance or monetary damages—in the case of a breach.

Advantages of Expert Support

Getting professional advice is highly encouraged because real estate transactions are difficult and entail legal nuances. The negotiation and drafting procedures could benefit substantially from the guidance of real estate attorneys or skilled legal consultants with a concentration on real estate law. They guarantee that contracts are detailed, preserve the interests of their clients, and are legally valid as they have considerable knowledge of local laws, regulations, and best practices.

There are various benefits to expert assistance

Legal Expertise: Specialists guarantee that contracts are legally sound and preserve their clients' interests by having a specialized grasp of real estate law, contract drafting, and negotiation.

Risk Mitigation: Experts carry out comprehensive due diligence, detect prospective threats, and insert proper provisions to safeguard their clients from unplanned occurrences or conflicts.

Customization of Contracts: Experts may draft contracts that are particularly suited to each transaction, taking into consideration the particulars of the property, the financing arrangements, and the preferences of the client.

Negotiation Skills: Expert negotiators can stand up for the interests of their clients by finding a middle ground between securing the best terms and retaining goodwill amongst the parties.

Comfort: Having specialists manage the contract process means that professionals are keeping an eye on things, which decreases the likelihood of errors or oversights.

In summary

To sum up, a successful real estate transaction relies on the negotiation and preparation of real estate contracts. Effective communication between all parties involved, legal awareness, and painstaking attention to detail are important. Both persons and companies may safeguard their interests, eliminate risks, and ensure a flawless and legally compliant real estate transaction by appreciating the relevance of efficient contract negotiations and drafting. Even if it is conceivable to conduct contract talks and drafting on your own, working with seasoned specialists like real estate attorneys or legal consultants may have a huge influence. These professionals have the knowledge, expertise, and negotiation talents required to properly handle intricate legal situations and preserve their clients' interests. They may aid in making sure that agreements are full, enforceable, and comply with all applicable regulations and laws. People and corporations may save time, keep out of trouble, and feel more at rest knowing that specialists are taking care of their legal difficulties by hiring professional aid. A real estate transaction may be considerably more effective and efficient when a trained professional is assisting you through terms and conditions analysis, due diligence, and dispute resolution. In summary, it is necessary to give serious thought to efficient contract talks and drafting before commencing a real estate enterprise. This provides the safety of all parties, the defining of all obligations, and the elimination of any potential threats. Individuals and companies may confidently traverse the intricate world of real estate transactions with the support of seasoned professionals, assuring a successful finish and ongoing success.

Chapter 8

The Whole Guide to Investing in Real Estate Financing

Investing in real estate may be done for several goals. Owning an investment property has various advantages and may function as a hedge against market volatility when stocks decrease.Purchasing an investment property is a great way to diversify your portfolio, whether you're holding onto land for future development, flipping a property, buying a property for an aging relative to live in and reaping the appreciation when it sells, or renting the property to generate passive income.Investing in real estate sometimes **includes a considerable start-up cost**, in contrast to investing in the stock market, which may be done for very little money. After you've done your investigation, concluded that real estate investing is the perfect route for you, and identified a reasonable deal, you'll need to consider financing your investment property. **Conventional bank loans, hard money loans, private money loans, and home equity loans are the four loan varieties you may utilize for investment properties.** There are numerous methods to finance investment properties, and borrowers must be able to fulfill specific standards. Before contacting a lender, make sure you understand the requirements of each sort of loan and how the various alternatives operate. Making the improper loan option could adversely affect the return on your investment.One option for financing investment properties is to leverage the equity in your home. It may be viable to employ the offered dollars if you don't have the money for a down payment on your own, but the monetary gifts need to be validated.Flipping refers to the process of acquiring properties and performing required improvements before reselling them for a profit.In comparison to typical mortgages, hard money loans frequently have a shorter payback tenure and operate as short-term finance. Hard money loans are not given by banks; only standard mortgages are.

Conventional Bank Loans

You most certainly already know what traditional financing is if you presently possess a house that acts as your primary dwelling. In contrast to loans from the Federal Home Administration (FHA), the Department of Veterans Affairs (VA), or the Department of Agriculture (USDA), a conventional mortgage conforms with restrictions established by Fannie Mae or Freddie Mac and is not insured by the federal government. 20% of the purchase price of the property is generally needed as a down payment when utilizing conventional financing. However, the lender might require a 30% down payment for an investment property. Your credit score and credit history affect both your loan approval status and the mortgage interest rate that will be paid on a typical loan. Lenders also look at the assets and income of borrowers. For an investment property, applicants need to show that they can afford both the monthly loan payments and their present mortgage. The debt-to-income (DTI) ratio does not account for potential rental earnings, and most lenders demand borrowers to have a minimum of six months' worth of cash on hand to satisfy both mortgage obligations.

Hard Money Loans

A hard money loan is a form of short-term loan that is best utilized for investment property flipping rather than acquiring, owning, renting, or developing real estate. While utilizing a hard money loan to acquire a property and immediately repaying it with a conventional loan, private money loan, or home equity loan is conceivable, it is more practical and inexpensive to start with one of the other choices if you do not want to flip your property. One benefit of financing a home flip using a hard money loan instead of a normal one is that the former may be more readily secured. Lenders still take creditworthiness and income into consideration, but the profitability of the property is their major concern. The estimated after-repair value (ARV) of the home is used to establish your capacity to repay the loan. In addition, loan money may be secured within a few days as compared to weeks or months for a standard mortgage closing. The biggest downside of employing a fix-and-flip hard money loan is its **high cost.** Depending on the lender, interest rates for this form of loan may exceed 18%, and payback periods might be limited. Hard money loans often come with terms shorter than a year. In addition, origination and closing charges might be larger than with standard financing, which can lower profits.

Loans for Private Money

Loans provided with private cash are granted by one individual to another. The bulk of loans obtained utilizing private money come from an investor's friends and family. Attending local real estate investment networking events is a good location to start looking for private money lenders if you don't have any friends or family who can lend you money for the purchase of an investment property. You may join local real estate investing clubs for networking reasons by checking out the directory kept by the well-known real estate investment podcast. Depending on the borrower-lender link, real loan terms and interest rates on private money loans may fluctuate widely, from very favorable to predatory. Usually, these loans are secured by a contract of some form, permitting the lender to take control of the property if you don't make your payments as promised. Before you sign an agreement with a loved one, if you're new to real estate investing, carefully evaluate how defaulting can harm your bond with the person who is to loan you the private money.

Using Your Home Equity

The fourth technique of getting an investment property is to leverage your home equity via a cash-out refinance, home equity line of credit (HELOC), or home equity loan. Generally speaking, you may borrow up to 80% of the equity in your residence to employ for investing in, purchasing, and fixing up a property.Depending on the sort of loan you pick, leveraging equity to support a real estate purchase provides benefits and downsides. For example, you may borrow against the equity in a HELOC in the same manner that you would with a credit card, and interest-only payments are frequently needed each month. However, as the rate is generally variable, it may rise in reaction to changes in the prime rate. Although a cash-out refinancing would have a fixed rate, it may help your existing mortgage last longer. Longer loan durations may result in higher interest rates for the primary residence. That would need to be considered against the projected revenue from an investment property.

What does it take to obtain financing for investment homes approved?

The requirements will fluctuate based on the lender and sort of finance. All that private lenders may require is a relationship with the borrower. A good estimated after-repair value (ARV) and a robust real estate market might be all that hard money lenders require. Lenders offering conventional loans, home equity lines of credit (HELOC), and home equity loans will impose the highest income and credit score conditions.Which is better for financing investment property. HELOCs and home equity loans are relatively similar products with some important variances. A home equity loan is a great alternative if you want to buy a single property and require an exact quantity of money for the purchase, repairs, and improvements. A home equity loan

(HELOC) is a more convenient alternative if you wish to buy and sell properties fast since it enables you to have revolving access to cash as you pay off your credit line with each purchase and sale, rather than taking out and repaying many home equity loans.

The Final Word

Although they entail some risk, rental property investments and home-flipping operations have the potential to deliver considerable rewards. If you know where to seek, you may quickly discover the money you need to take advantage of an investment opportunity. Consider the short- and long-term expenditures connected with each borrowing decision and how they may affect the total return on your investment when you compare them. The way we experience homes is changing due to virtual reality property tours. Technology has grabbed the lead in the quick-paced real estate sector, drastically transforming how we view, acquire, and manage houses. VR property tours are one innovation that is generating a stir in the industry. By allowing prospective renters and buyers to tour properties without ever setting foot inside, these immersive experiences are transforming the real estate market. Have you ever been presented with the annoying situation of skimming through real estate listings and not being able to view the property beyond still photographs and descriptions? You're not alone yourself.This is a difficulty that many would-be renters and buyers experience when shopping for their dream residence. Virtual Reality (VR) property tours are a revolutionary method that is altering the way we perceive real estate. Technology has grabbed the lead in the quick-paced real estate sector, drastically transforming how we view, acquire, and manage houses. VR property tours are one innovation that is generating a stir in the industry. By allowing prospective renters and buyers to tour properties without ever setting foot inside, these immersive experiences are transforming the real estate market. In this book section, we'll address this frequent problem and explain how virtual reality technology provides a solution that will alter the real estate industry and enhance everyone's experience when acquiring or renting a property.

A Novel Approach to Home Exploration

The days of navigating via two-dimensional floor layouts and static images are long gone. Virtual reality (VR) property tours give potential renters or buyers with a dynamic, 360-degree picture of a property, giving them a realistic idea of its layout and scale. From the comfort of your own home, envision yourself entering a neatly furnished living room, strolling through the kitchen, and peering into the bedrooms. With virtual reality, experiencing is more crucial than merely seeing.

<u>Conserving Money and Time</u>

The potential of virtual reality property tours to save time and money for both buyers and sellers is one of its largest advantages. You no longer need to plan many in-person property visits, which occasionally take place over several weekends. You may "visit" numerous houses in a single day using virtual reality. This expedites the search process and makes it simpler for renters and consumers to pick what they want. VR tours minimize interruptions to merchants' routine schedules. Rather than having to routinely organize their properties for showings, they may engage someone to design a virtual reality tour, which may be experienced by multiple potential renters or purchases. Those who are selling vacant or remote residences would especially profit from this.

<u>The Increase in Remote Home Purchases</u>

Virtual reality property tours are transformative for investors and faraway buyers. Virtual reality tours are a terrific method to examine residences without having to travel regularly if you're relocating to a different city or even country. Due to greater accessibility, cross-border real estate transactions are now simpler to conduct and less stressful. Real estate markets are more accessible to a larger public.

<u>Individualization and Tailoring</u>

Virtual reality property tours also provide the option for personalization and customization. Renters and purchasers may choose to focus on the things that are most essential to them or take their time investigating every inch of a house. To make sure they haven't neglected anything, they could even return to their residences multiple times.

The Function of Real Estate Brokers

Additionally utilizing VR technology are real estate salesmen. They may remotely guide consumers through virtual reality tours while delivering informative commentary and immediately responding to concerns. Even in cases where agents and clients are unable to be in the same physical area, this degree of participation encourages increased communication and trust between them.

Overcoming Difficulties

Virtual reality property tours offer a lot of potential, but they also have major downsides. Not everyone can employ VR headsets or has the appropriate technical expertise. To reach a larger audience, some virtual reality tour operators do, however, also offer web-based or mobile app versions of their tours.

<u>The Prospects for Real Estate</u>

More exciting improvements in the real estate sector are inevitable as VR technology improves. The possibilities are infinite, ranging from virtual reality neighborhood tours to VR staging that allows customers to modify the look of a property. Virtual reality property tours give a peek into the future of real estate, not merely a fad. In summary, virtual reality property tours have had a profoundly transformative influence on the real estate business. Property research is now simpler to access, more accessible, and more fun owing to these immersive experiences that bridge the gap between dream and reality. We could anticipate even more inventive VR uses in the real estate business as technology evolves. The possibilities are intriguing, with interactive neighborhood tours and virtual staging among them. Thus, it's time to embrace the digital revolution and join the future of real estate, one virtual tour at a time, whether you're a buyer, seller, or real estate professional.

Chapter 9

What Virtual Real Estate Have In-Store

How will virtual real estate fare in the future?

Although the idea of virtual real estate has been around for a while, it has just recently started to acquire steam as a feasible business model. What is virtual real estate, and is it something your firm should consider selling? To put it simply, virtual real estate is a property that exists online. Websites, blogs, social media accounts, or even individual blog entries may be instances of this. Virtual real estate provides a chance to benefit from this rising trend, even if the physical world still plays a vital part in our lives.There are various reasons why your firm has to look at selling virtual property for sale. It's a terrific approach to generate passive money, to start with. After collecting a collection of virtual assets, you may begin to generate money via sponsorships, advertising, or even direct sales. Additionally, the profit potential is fairly excellent due to the incredibly low overhead costs (you don't have to worry about things like property taxes or maintenance). Selling virtual real estate is a superb way to create your brand, which is another incentive to do so. You can make sure that your brand shows at the top of search results for products or services in your industry by holding strong digital real estate. Additionally, you have a high opportunity of getting in early and becoming the market leader as virtual real estate is still a relatively new notion.

Of course, selling virtual real estate has inherent pitfalls of its own. There's no promise that the space will develop at the same fast speed as it has in recent years given it's still so new. Furthermore, you might find yourself owning a lot of worthless virtual property if the market does tumble.Nevertheless, your firm should consider about selling virtual real estate as the rewards transcend the hazards. You may start producing passive income for years to come by joining a fresh and intriguing market with a little amount of preparation and planning.

<u>How Can Virtual Real Estate Be Sold?</u>

The way we conduct business has been radically affected by the Internet. Businesses used to make considerable expenditures in physical shops. However, an increasing number of enterprises are now functioning online. A new sort of real estate has evolved as a consequence of this change: virtual real estate.A property that exists online is known as virtual real estate. Websites, domain names, and even internet organizations could come under this category. Virtual real estate may be just as valuable as traditional real estate, yet not having the same physical presence. A few considerations should be addressed if you wish to sell virtual real estate.

<u>*1. Calculate the Property's Value*</u>

Finding the value of the virtual property is the first step in selling it. You'll need to take into consideration numerous aspects, such as the property's location, traffic, and revenue possibilities. To evaluate the traffic and income potential of a website, apply tools such as Alexa and Google Analytics. You may begin offering the house to prospective consumers as soon as you have a clear grip on its value.

2. Identify the Proper Purchaser

Every consumer is not created evenly. You want to identify a buyer who is a suitable fit for the property when selling virtual real estate. Selling a website that specializes in home decoration, for instance, would be best suited for a buyer with interest in that area. This also applies to domain names. Seek a buyer who works in the fashion industry if you are selling a fashion-related domain name.

3. Discuss the Sale

It's time to negotiate the sale of your property when you've located a buyer who exhibits interest. It will be beneficial in this circumstance to have a strong notion of the property's value. Make sure to start high and be open to make compromises during haggling. It's also vital to know precisely how much you're willing to accept for the sale of the house. You may continue with the deal after you and the buyer have agreed on a price.

4. Finalize the Purchase

It's time to complete the transaction after you've negotiated it. The buyer normally acquires ownership of the property as a consequence of this. This generally means relocating the domain name and website files for websites and online companies. This requires altering the DNS records for domain names to reflect the new owner. One of the finest methods to generate money from your online assets is to sell virtual real estate. These ideas will help you boost your chances of success.

Who Will Purchase Virtual Property?

Yes, your organization has to consider selling virtual property for sale. This is the reason why:

1. The market for virtual real estate is booming.

The demand for virtual real estate is expanding as more and more enterprises turn to operating online. An increasing number of firms are seeking for techniques to have an online presence, and they want a location to host their online shop or website.

2. One fantastic technique to make money is via virtual real estate.

Selling virtual real estate is a terrific approach for your organization to gain money. Businesses wishing to build an online presence may acquire virtual property from you, or you may offer virtual space to enterprises looking to operate an online store or website.

3. A fantastic investment is virtual real estate.

For your company, virtual real estate is a wonderful investment. It's a market that is developing and has a good potential to generate money. You may gain when the corporation that acquires your virtual land builds on it or sells it later if you sell it. When a corporation acquires virtual space from you and uses it to host their website or online store, you will profit.

4. Selling virtual real estate is straightforward.

It's easy to sell virtual real estate. You have two alternatives for selling your property: either post it on online marketplaces or sell it directly to enterprises that require virtual space.

5. *Virtual real estate is a wonderful tool for company advertising.*

One of the finest methods to market your company is to offer virtual real estate. Businesses that acquire virtual property or space from you are receiving visibility for their company. This can aid you in extending your clients and developing your organization.

Which sort of virtual property is the most valuable?

Many different forms of property may be acquired and sold in the virtual real estate market. But not every virtual property is built equally. Virtual real estate occurs in numerous kinds, and the changes in its prices are typically the consequence of a confluence of events.

The location of virtual real estate is one of the essential components that determines its value. When it comes to virtual real estate, location is vital, just as in the real world. In general, houses in well-liked, bustling locations are worth more than those in less desirable ones. This is because properties in well-known districts have a better chance of being viewed by potential buyers and also have a propensity to improve in value over time.

The sort of property is a crucial extra component that determines the value of virtual real estate. For instance, properties used for corporate reasons are typically valued more than ones used for household consumption. This is because commercial real estate frequently brings in more money than residential real estate. Commercial properties are also commonly placed in attractive regions, which enhances their price even more. Lastly, the sort of virtual environment a piece of virtual real estate is placed in may influence its value. For instance, properties in virtual worlds meant for social networking or enjoyment tend to be less valuable than those in virtual worlds intended for commerce or trade. This is a consequence of the greater chance that enterprises and other organizations would employ virtual worlds for their operations and their increased readiness to pay for real estate placed in these sorts of worlds.

What form of virtual property is therefore the most valuable?

It depends on numerous criteria, such as the property's location, type, and sort of virtual environment. But generally speaking, the most desirable properties are those that are employed for business and are located in busy, well-traveled districts.

8. Why Does Real Estate Gross Matter?

Given the great profitability of the real estate industry, investors are continually exploring tactics to maximize their profits. The gross acres are one of the criteria that matter a lot when investing in real estate. The complete land area of a property, including all of the buildings, roads, and other structures, is measured in gross acres. In real estate, gross acres are essential for various reasons, which we will cover here.

1. Property Appraisal

A property's gross acres have a substantial influence on its value. The value of the land grows with the gross acreage. This is because larger properties can house more buildings or structures and have higher development potential. A 10-acre lot that can contain 100 apartments, for instance, is worth more than a 5-acre site that can only hold 50 units.

2. Possibility of Development

A property's potential for development is also evaluated by its gross acres. bigger gross acreage correlates to higher potential income as it gives more room for development. To enhance revenue sources, a significant gross area of land could be turned into an industrial park, commercial center, or subdivision.

3. Segmentation

Zoning restrictions are also highly impacted by gross acres. Zoning rules outline the sorts of structures that are authorized in an area, the number of units that may be developed there, and the kinds of activities that are permitted there. Greater zoning flexibility may be feasible on a site with a higher gross area, allowing for extra development alternatives.

4. Use in Agriculture

When considering a property's potential for agricultural utilization, gross acres are also significant. Additional income streams may be created by farming, ranching, or other agricultural interests on a property with a higher gross acreage. To enhance revenue streams, a 50-acre property may be employed for livestock production or crops.

<u>5. Availability</u>

The accessibility of a property is also dictated by its gross acres. A property with a bigger gross area may be simpler to access, allowing more opportunity for expansion and income generation. A vast gross acreage property near an airport, major highway, or other transportation hub, for instance, might be simpler to access and give more investment chances. When investing in real estate, gross acres count. higher expansion potential, better property value, more opportunity for agricultural use, and more accessibility are all related to a wider gross acreage property. To maximize profits and investment possibilities, gross acres of land must be taken into consideration when making real estate investments.

What benefits does venture capital bring to private investors in real estate

Venture capital advantages include private venture capital, private real estate, and real estate investors. An important source of cash for many small and fledgling firms is venture capital. Venture money may also benefit private real estate investors, particularly those who seek to develop their company or purchase other properties. Typically, venture capital companies support enterprises that have considerable growth potential but are too risky for banks or other traditional lenders. This form of investment may aid private real estate investors in collecting the capital necessary to acquire new properties, make modifications to existing ones, or even start new companies. The capacity of venture capital to give the money necessary to embark on greater undertakings is one of its key benefits. For instance, venture capital may be used to finance the purchase of a new property if an investor intends to buy one but lacks the requisite finances.Venture capital also helps investors diversify their , which is another benefit. Investors may minimize their overall risk by making investments in a range of businesses.Mentorship and assistance may also be gained effectively from venture capital. With their significant understanding of the real estate market, a huge number of venture capitalists may supply investors with informative guidance. Naturally, there are hazards related to venture capital as well. The risk that the firm fails and the investor loses all of their money is one of the major hazards. Do your study and be informed of all the prospective hazards and advantages before making any sort of investment. Although it's not ideal for everyone, venture capital may be a superb choice to support your real estate ambitions.

For private real estate investors, what are the risks involved with venture capital?

Venture capital hazards include those associated with private venture capital, private real estate, and real estate investors.Although it could be harmful, real estate has long been a popular investment. While there are particular dangers unique to venture capital that private real estate investors must be cautious of, they also face many of the same risks as any other sort of investor.The potential of losing principle is one of the key hazards connected with venture funding. Although every investment has some risk, venture capital investments are frequently regarded as having a bigger risk than other forms of investments. This suggests that investors have a larger possibility of losing all or part of their original investment. An additional risk associated with venture capital is the investment's lack of liquidity. The difficulty of venture capital investments to be quickly turned into cash can make it difficult for investors to exit their holdings should the situation arise. This may be particularly troublesome if the money is put in a nascent firm that isn't yet listed on the stock market. Lastly, when investing in venture capital, private real estate investors should be wary of the possibility of conflicts of interest. Venture capitalists may be more tempted to act against the best interests of the company or its shareholders since they are generally more concerned with earning a profit than with developing the enterprise. For instance, even when it is not in the best interests of the company or its workers, a venture investor may insist on the firm being sold so they may benefit from their investment.Even while venture capital has inherent disadvantages, it could still be a smart alternative for individual real estate investors. Investors may enhance their chances of success by being aware of the risks and taking appropriate measures to mitigate them.

What is the best strategy for private real estate investors to exploit venture capital opportunities

Venture capital options for private real estate investors in private real estate. The following advice is something private real estate investors might consider to optimize their venture capital opportunities:

Have a well-defined investment thesis

It's vital to have a short and comprehensible investment thesis before approaching any probable venture capitalists. This should contain your target markets, the sort of property or properties you want to invest in, and the projected return on your investment. It will be easier to convey your investment opportunity to venture capitalists (VCs) and more probable that you will acquire funding if you have a well-defined thesis.

★ **Before pitching your investment plan to potential venture capitalists, it is vital that you undertake complete research on them. This means knowing about their investing needs and researching their portfolio and investment history. This will provide you with a better notion of how to construct your pitch in addition to aiding you in selecting whether a specific VC is a great fit for your chance.**

Be ready to give up equity

It's vital to be ready to give up ownership of your firm when soliciting venture capital financing. When participating in conversations, it's vital to be at peace with the typical structure of venture capitalists (VCs) issuing shares in exchange for investments in early-stage firms. Lastly, it is crucial to have a good business plan in place before obtaining venture capital financing. This ought to contain detailed financial predictions as well as a grasp of the risks and obstacles your firm confronts. Convincing VCs to invest in your startup will be tough if you don't have a convincing business plan.

Use Software for Specialized Real Estate Analysis

Specialized real estate analysis software could be a wonderful solution for investors who have a big real estate portfolio or who want more in-depth study. These systems feature characteristics like automated rolling returns calculations, adjustable reporting, and connection with other financial metrics as they are specifically built to handle the nuances of real estate investment. Even while these software packages are frequently pricey, they may save a lot of time and effort for investors, freeing them up to focus on making better-informed investment decisions.

Think About the Best Choice

Rolling returns for real estate investments may be estimated using spreadsheet tools or by hand, but employing professional real estate analysis software provides various advantages. These software tools decrease errors, streamline the workflow, and give complete analytical features. Additionally, they generally come with added tools like scenario modeling, risk assessment, and portfolio optimization, which help investors thoroughly appreciate their real estate holdings. Consequently, obtaining specialized software is suggested for investors who wish to boost efficiency and acquire a better knowledge of their real estate assets.Investors may analyze their real estate assets effectively by recognizing the principle of rolling returns, picking the proper rolling period, and applying the applicable instruments. The ability to calculate rolling returns, whether by manual calculations, spreadsheet programs, or specialized software, gives crucial insights into the performance of real estate assets and, in the end, assists with decision-making regarding investments.

Chapter 9

What is the income from real estate?

It is income obtained from real estate ownership or

investment. This may include interest and dividends obtained from real estate investments, rental income, and revenues from the sale of real estate.Real estate revenue comes in several ways, **but the two most prominent are revenues from the sale of real estate and rental income.** Profits from selling property are the money you make when you sell your home or investment property, whereas rental income is the money you obtain by renting out your property.Profits from the sale of real estate as well as the rental income are taxed, therefore it's necessary to keep correct records and disclose this money on your tax return. Gaining money from real estate investments may enhance your take-home income and help you create wealth over time. Additionally, it may be a fairly passive source of income that offers you retirement financial security if you prepare and employ the necessary strategies. Make sure you investigate the different sources of real estate income if you're contemplating investing in real estate. Real estate investment may be a sensible technique to gain money and preserve your financial future with a little planning and research.

What weight are dividends and income from earnings from real estate?

Dividends and income from real estate are both treated as taxable. There are some differences between the two, however. When a dividend is received, it is recognized as taxable income. This indicates that you will be liable for paying taxes on dividends you obtain if you own shares in a company. When earned, hobby money is recognized as taxable income. This indicates that you will have to pay taxes on any money you gain from a hobby. Dividends and income from hobbies have certain connections. Both forms of income are treated as taxable. There are some differences between the two, however. When a dividend is received, it is recognized as taxable income. This indicates that you will be liable for paying taxes on dividends you obtain if you own shares in a company. When earned, hobby money is recognized as taxable income. This indicates that you will have to pay taxes on any money you gain from a hobby

Advantages of Real Estate Investing

Buying real estate provides several benefits. The following are some of the most popular explanations stated by investors for investing in this asset class.

Portfolio diversification

Investing in real estate could benefit in diversifying your assets. You may lower your overall risk and enhance your chances of accomplishing your financial goals by placing investments in a different asset class.

Stability

Investing in real estate is fairly stable. Values of real estate frequently move less over time than those of stocks and other securities. Those looking to make long-term investments may find peace of mind in this stability.

Income

The rental payments obtained from real estate investments may be a steady source of income. Your retirement years may be financially secure with this income, which may also help to supplement your other sources of income.

Tax benefits

Investing in real estate provides various tax advantages. These benefits may include interest deductions on mortgages, real estate taxes, and other expenditures.

Equity growth

The value of your house will undoubtedly increase with time. Equity expansion, the word for this value growth, may be leveraged to support further objectives or investments, such as a down payment on a second house.

Leverage

You may apply leverage to support your real estate deal when you invest. Using debt to support an enterprise is known as leverage. This suggests that a lower down payment will enable you to obtain a larger property.

Cost-effective

Compared to many other asset classes, real estate is a more cost-effective investment. Because of its affordability, investing in real estate and accomplishing financial goals is made easy for investors.

Control

Compared to other sorts of investments, real estate investing provides you greater control over your money. Both the property you wish to invest in and the amount you are willing to pay are up to you. To boost the property's value, you may also renovate or make other modifications.

Advantages of Real Estate Investing

Real estate investing has risen in popularity over the past few years across all skill levels of investors. And with good reason—real estate investing offers numerous evident advantages.

Consistency and Foreseeability

The regularity and predictability that real estate investing may bring is one of its key benefits. The real estate market is far more stable and predictable than the stock market, which is prone to quick and dramatic shifts. There will always be highs and lows, of course, but values normally climb steadily over time to give a significant return on investment.

Material Good

Investing in a tangible asset is one of the key benefits of real estate investment. In contrast to stocks and bonds, which are paper documents (or digital records), real estate is a physical asset that is in your hands. For some investors, this could create a better sense of security and comfort.

Utilize

Leveraging your investment is another advantage of real estate investing. Using other people's money to support your enterprise is known as leverage. When investing in real estate, you can generally finance the remaining amount with a mortgage after making a small down payment—sometimes as little as 10%. This provides you with relatively little money in return for control over a substantially bigger asset.

Cash Movement

The cash flow that real estate investing may bring is one of its strongest benefits. Tenant payments are given to you every month when you invest in rental properties. If you own enough properties, this may become your full-time source of income or an excellent addition to it.

Benefits of Taxation

The significant tax benefits that come with real estate investing are another plus. For instance, you may lower your taxable income by deducting the interest you pay on your mortgage. To further minimize your tax bill, you may additionally depreciate the value of your property (a technique known as "cost recovery").

Creating Wealth

Ultimately, the capacity to steadily amass money is among the most fundamental benefits of real estate investing. Your equity, or the proportion of your house that you own, will increase when the value of your property rises and your mortgage debt reduces. And you may even speed up this process if you reinvest your rental money properly.These are just a handful of the numerous perks that come with real estate investing. The first thing you should examine while seeking a reliable investment with lots of potential is real estate. The possibility for long-term gain is one of the primary benefits of real estate investing. In other words, a property that you acquire for $100,000 may be worth $120,000 or more in a few years. There are various explanations for this appreciation, including market demand and inflation. Real estate may therefore be a good long-term investment. The possibility for a good return on investment (ROI) is another benefit of real estate investing. This indicates the fraction of the original investment that is recouped following the sale of the property. The ROI would be 20%, for instance, if an investor acquired a property for $100,000 and sold it for $120,000. By adding renovations and alterations to the property, which enhance its value, ROI may be further improved. Lastly, rental income from real estate may be a solid source of income. When you purchase a property and rent it out, your tenant will pay you regularly. This may generate a considerable passive income that may aid in alleviating the cost of any linked costs, such as a mortgage.

Risks connected with real estate investing

There are various significant risks involved with real estate investing that you should be aware of. A few of the things that could go wrong are as follows:

1. There's a danger the residence may lose value.

A piece of real estate may rise or decrease in value, just like any other asset. You might lose money on your investment if you purchase a property and its market value lowers.

2. It might be challenging to find tenants.

There is always a danger that you won't be able to attract tenants if you want to rent out your residence. This might require you to remain paying monthly expenditures for a home you are unable to sell.

3. It's conceivable for you to be sued.

You might find yourself sued if something goes wrong with your property, such as a tenant getting harmed. Even if you win the case, this can end up costing you a lot of money.

4. You may become a victim of foreclosure.

The bank may foreclose on your property if you are unable to pay your mortgage. This would suggest that you would lose both your home and the total amount of money you placed into the property.

5. There might be concerns with the property itself.

There's always the potential that troubles with the property itself may occur, even if everything else goes as expected. You might have structural, plumbing, or electrical concerns, for instance. You might lose money on your investment as addressing any of these difficulties could be pricey. You can assess if real estate investing is suitable for you now that you are aware of some of the concerns involved. Real estate investing may be a superb approach to gaining some money if you're willing to take on these hazards. You may want to consider picking another investment decision, however, if you're not comfortable taking on these dangers.

If you're contemplating it, there are a few things you should know beforehand. Potential investors should be aware of many pitfalls when it comes to real estate investing. These dangers may be loosely split into two groups: risks linked to money and risks related to health.Risks related to money include things like the chance for property value to drop or rent default by the tenant. Physical threats include things like a natural catastrophe destroying or harming property. Naturally, there is risk connected with any investment, and there's always a potential that anything may go wrong. You may, however, make intelligent decisions and pick assets that are right for you if you are aware of the potential pitfalls connected with real estate investment.

Chapter 10

What is Real Estate Civilization

The process of assessing a property's valuation is known as "localization" in real estate. It is an important component of the real estate market as it promotes informed decision-making for lenders, buyers, and sellers. The market value of a property is defined by its degree of civilization, and this may affect the selling price, rental income, and mortgage rates. This chapter of "virtual real estate gold", will go over the concept of real estate appraisal, its relevance, and the different methodologies used to assess a property's value.

What is Real Estate Civilization?

The process of finding out a property's value is civilization.Investing in real estate may be transformed by civilization. With the assistance of this tool, investors may estimate a property's potential value and decide on their next step with certainty. This technique comprises examining a property's location, size, condition, and other aspects that determine its valuation. Numerous elements, including demand, market fluctuations, and the status of the economy, may impact a property's value. In the real estate market, the aviation process is vital as it promotes intelligent decision-making for lenders, buyers, and sellers.

The Value of Assessment in Real Estate

The degree of civilization has a substantial influence on a property's market value. The price a property would sell for in a competitive market is its market value. To ensure such a property is valued effectively, it is vital to assess its market worth. Underpricing a property could result in missed potential revenue while overpricing it might lead it to stay on the market for longer. Lenders also apply this to analyze a property's valuation before issuing mortgage loans.

Real Estate Techniques

The sales comparison method, the cost approach, and the income approach are the three basic approaches used to assess a property's value. Comparing the property to similar properties that have recently sold in the area is part of the sales comparison approach. With the cost technique, depreciation is taken into account and the cost of replacing the property in the case of its destruction is determined. For commercial assets, the income approach is employed, which comprises estimating the probable revenue the property may produce.

Examining and comparing the three methods

The sales comparison approach is the most widely utilized tool for residential properties. This technique is advised since it is straightforward to interpret and delivers a clear impression of the property's value. When comparing a property's distinguishing traits to those of other properties in the region, the cost approach is applied. For commercial assets, the income method is employed, and it is premised on the probable revenue that the property may produce. Nevertheless, this strategy may be tough and demands a comprehensive grasp of the sector and the probable income the property may bring.Finding a property's market value assists in the decision-making process for lenders, buyers, and sellers. The sales comparison method, the cost approach, and the income approach are the three basic approaches used to assess a property's value. Every technique has pros and downsides, and the most suited strategy will differ based on the property being appraised.

How Will Civilization Change the Real Estate Investment Landscape?

1. Provides right property assessment

Correct property value is one of civilization most essential features. To offer an accurate evaluation, this tool evaluates various aspects, including the property's location, size, and condition. As a consequence, investors are better able to decide on the prospective value of a property and the possible returns on their investment.

2. Time and money saved

Real estate investors may save a tremendous lot of time and money by employing civilization. Investors would have to spend a tremendous lot of time and money examining and analyzing a property without this tool. This technique is mechanized by realization, which delivers investors trustworthy and exact information in a matter of minutes. This tool offers investors a clear image of the future value of a property, which helps them avoid pricey blunders.

3. Another benefit of Civilization is that it enables investors to uncover alternatives that may be veiled from view. Significant amounts of data, such as historical sales, rental rates, and real estate trends, may be evaluated using this tool to locate properties that are inexpensive or have the potential to make big profits. By doing this, investors may be able to find prospects that they may have overlooked otherwise.

4. Civilization gives a competitive advantage

Real estate investors may acquire an edge by employing civilization. Investors may react quicker to opportunities and make better choices when they have access to clear and trustworthy information. By doing this, investors may be able to beat the competition and enhance the return on their investments.

5. Ultimately, investors may limit risk by employing avalanche analysis. With the capacity to appropriately evaluate assets and find hidden potential, this tool may aid investors in making well-informed selections that decrease risk. By doing this, investors may lower their risk and enhance the return on their cash. Investing in real estate may be transformed by civilization. Accurate property evaluations are supplied, time and money are saved, investors are given a competitive advantage, hidden opportunities are identified, and risk is decreased. Real estate investors may boost their returns on investment and make better decisions by utilizing this tool.

<u>Real Estate and Real Money in Real Estate and Investments</u>

There are a few things you can do to lower the expense of your real estate investments. Start by searching for properties that are undervalued or in need of repair. As a consequence of their generally below-market price, these homes will enable you to receive a beneficial deal. Using creative financing solutions is another alternative to minimize the cost of your assets. For instance, you may purchase a property utilizing seller financing. This can result in big financial savings for you as there won't be a down payment necessary when you buy the property. Try bargaining with the merchants as well. You may save money on your investment if you can convince a seller to decrease their asking price. Lastly, if you're not obtaining what you want out of a deal, don't be frightened to walk away. Don't waste time on a house that isn't a good fit for you because there are always other properties available.

SUMMARY

"Virtual Real Estate Gold" by Jeffrey S Loomis is a pioneering guide that sheds light on the remarkable potential of virtual wholesaling in the digital age. The book explores how virtual wholesaling allows individuals to conduct real estate transactions with minimal physical presence, leveraging digital technologies such as the web, email, digital signatures, and smartphones. It delves into the benefits of virtual wholesaling, such as the freedom of location and the ability to operate in multiple markets from anywhere in the world. The book emphasizes the growing significance of virtual wholesaling in the real estate investment industry, highlighting the lucrative opportunities it presents for aspiring entrepreneurs and seasoned investors alike. Through the firsthand experiences of successful real estate entrepreneurs like Alex Martinez and Ryan Zomorodi, the book offers valuable insights into the transformative power of virtual wholesaling and its potential to revolutionize one's approach to real estate investment. With a step-by-step guide to virtual wholesaling, practical tips, **"Virtual Real Estate Gold"** equips readers with the knowledge and strategies needed to thrive in the evolving landscape of real estate investment. Whether you're looking to make a foray into virtual wholesaling or seeking to enhance your existing real estate ventures, this book is a compelling resource that unveils the secrets to succeeding in the dynamic realm of digital real estate.